"A 'must have' for any amateur or profe[ssional]
about gardening, farm-to-table, organi[c]

—*Sante*

"…Rich personal stories, useful tips for canning and storing,
and smartly written, eminently approachable small-batch recipes
leave us hard-pressed to find so much as a single fruit, vegetable,
or herb that doesn't work beautifully in a jar."

—*Saveur*

"I'm delighted that McClellan's Food in Jars blog is now a book…
[it's] not restricted to jams and pickles;
it's also got everything from nut butters to salsas."

—*Seattle Times*

"McClellan's voice is friendly and reassuring; the batches are manageable.
True to its name, this recipe collection covers territory beyond the ping of a
sealed lid, such as salts, syrups, granolas, stocks and butters."

—*Washington Post*

preserving
by the
PINT

preserving
by the
PINT

Quick Seasonal Canning for Small Spaces
by the author of **food** *in* **jars**

Marisa McClellan

RUNNING PRESS
PHILADELPHIA · LONDON

ISBN 978-0-7624-4968-2

Library of Congress Control Number: 2013943528

E-book ISBN 978-0-7624-5180-7

9   8   7   6   5   4   3   2   1

Digit on the right indicates the number of this printing

Cover and interior design by Amanda Richmond

Edited by Kristen Green Wiewora

Typography: Clarendon, Helvetica Neue, and New Cuisine

Running Press Book Publishers
2300 Chestnut Street
Philadelphia, PA 19103-4371

Visit us on the web!
www.offthemenublog.com

This book is dedicated
to my husband, Scott.
Neither this volume, nor my
career as a food writer, would
exist without his endless
love, encouragement,
and support.

This cookbook is for people who
live in cities and have tiny kitchens.
It's for newlyweds, empty nesters, and other households
of just one or two. It's for CSA subscribers who love
supporting their local farmers but who struggle to eat through
their share each week. It's for parents who want to get their
young kids involved in canning, but can't keep short attention
spans focused for more than ten minutes. It's for gardeners
with postage-stamp-size plots and for farmers' market
regulars. And it's for anyone who wants to dip a toe
into the world of food preservation.
Maybe it's for you.

Contents

INTRODUCTION

When I first started canning, I made huge batches of jam. Between the cleaning, peeling, and chopping, I'd be dripping with sweat and every inch of my kitchen would be covered in sticky fruit residue. Despite the fact that each jamming session took hours and hours, I did it that way because that's just how I thought canning was supposed to be. After all, every traditional recipe I found yielded five or seven or nine pints of jam. I just didn't see how it could be done any other way.

However, at the end of that first year, I discovered that even after eating jam on a daily basis and giving away many, many jars, I was still swimming in preserves. I knew that I really enjoyed the process of putting up, so giving it up until the first year's jams were gone wasn't an option. I needed to find a way for it to take less time and yield smaller amounts.

And so I started tearing down the recipes, dividing the amount of produce required and finding pieces of cookware that worked best with these small batches. I also developed techniques for breaking up the work, so that I could do it when it was most convenient for me without sacrificing freshness.

These days, I do a lot of very small batches. The jams, jellies, and chutneys yield just two or three half-pint jars, as do my batches of pickles. I also do a lot of preserving that doesn't include the canning pot at all, but instead are simply designed to buy me a few extra days or weeks with a bundle of herbs or a dry quart of Kirby cucumbers. Preserving on this scale means that I get to explore different flavor combinations without ever committing massive amounts of produce to an idea that might not work out. It also allows me to have three or four dozen different kinds of jams, conserves, and sauces in my pantry. I really enjoy having that kind of breadth and I have a feeling that there are a lot of other people who might just appreciate it as well.

TECHNIQUE

There are a number of very handy things about preserving in small batches. Because you're only dealing with modest quantity of produce, the preparation goes fast. What's more, a number of the recipes call for you to let the fruit sit and rest for a time with the sweetener after you're done peeling and chopping and pitting. If you've run out of time on that particular day, it's at this point that you can cover your bowl and pop the fruit into the fridge to macerate for 12 to 24 hours. They also cook quickly, particularly if you use wide pans. Best of all, because we're cooking in such small batches, these preserves tend to be lower in added sugar than are more conventional recipes, because you just don't need as much to sugar to support the set.

COOKWARE

There are just three pieces of cookware that I really recommend if want to do these tiny batches. The first is a basic, 12-inch (30.5 cm) stainless-steel skillet. This is an amazing pan for cooking small batches of jam. The wide base gives the fruit a lot of surface area on which to cook and the short, sloped sides encourage evaporation. Four cups/910 g of combined fruit and sugar take just 7 or 8 minutes to cook to a jammy consistency in a wide skillet.

Stainless steel, anodized aluminum, or enameled cast iron are the best materials to choose for these acidic preserves because they won't leach metallic flavors into your jam. Cast iron and aluminum can give jam a tinny taste. Nonstick is acceptable, but I find that it's much harder to tell when batches of jam are nearing completion on a nonstick surface.

For some of the slightly larger batches, or for recipes that cook down longer, I find that a 5-quart /4.8-liter Dutch oven is a really good pot for the job. You don't have to get a fancy enameled one: I have an inexpensive stainless-steel version that is perfectly sturdy.

The final piece of cookware that makes for easy small batches is a tall, skinny pot, preferably fitted with a rack. Asparagus pots do the job nicely, but my favorite is what Kuhn Rikon calls a 4TH burner pot. It works well as either a processing pot (you can fit either two wide-mouth or three Ball Collection Elite half-pint/250 ml jars in it) or as a pot for heating up pickling liquid. Thanks to the pour spout and coated handle, you can heat the vinegar in it and then pour directly into the prepared jars. I am very fond of this little pot. When it comes to processing slightly larger batches, an 8-quart/7.6-liter nonreactive stockpot fitted with a stainless-steel rack on the bottom does the job. The most important thing is that it's deep enough so that the jars are fully submerged with an inch/2.5 ml of water covering them, with room for the water to boil. The jars should not rest directly on the bottom of the pot, as the direct heat could cause them to crack. What's more, the rack permits the water to circulate around the jars, which allows for complete heat penetration and sterilization.

You'll also want to have a small saucepan on hand for simmering the lids. Anything you've got in your kitchen is just fine. Standard canning jars in the United States are three-part contraptions. You've got a jar, a ring (also known as a band), and the flat metal lid. Embedded in every lid is a strip of sealing compound that must be softened prior to use. To soften that compound, you simply simmer the lids in a small saucepan of water for 10 minutes or so (try not to boil them if you can manage it). Do remember that lids can only be used once for canning (if you soften a couple too many during canning prep, they can be used again. They just can't be sealed to a jar and then reused).

OTHER TOOLS

In addition to your pots, it's helpful to have several measuring cups on hand. I like having a few larger-capacity, heat-resistant (such as Pyrex) cups around, as well as a stainless-steel 1-cup/250 ml measure (so handy for filling 1-pint/500 ml and half-pint/250 ml) jars.

As far as specialized canning tools go, I find two particularly useful. The first is a wide-mouth funnel and the second is a jar lifter. Although you don't have to have either of these tools, they will make your canning life significantly easier. The magnetic lid lift that comes in most canning tool kits is also nifty but by no means essential.

Beyond that, a few other tools are nice to have, which I will reference on occasion in my recipes. Included in that list are a sharp paring knife, a serrated-edge peeler, a Microplane zester, a candy thermometer, a splatter shield, a fine-mesh strainer, an inexpensive mandoline, and an immersion blender.

THE WHYS OF PROCESSING PRESERVES

Many of the recipes included in this book are designed for boiling water bath canning. This is the process in which filled jars are submerged in a pot of boiling water and simmered for a prescribed amount of time. This is also the step that scares most people off from canning, as they think it is messy, time consuming, or dangerous. But as with so many kitchen tasks, after you've done it once or twice, it will lose its intimidation factor.

It is important not to skip the boiling-water process, as it performs two tasks and does both exceedingly well. First, boiling the filled jars kills any contaminants that might have landed in your jars (keep in mind that this processing method only works with high-acid foods. More about that in a minute). Second, the oxygen in the headspace is heated sufficiently to make it expand and push its way out of the jar. Once you remove the jar from the hot water, the jar will cool, the space will contract, and the lid will pull down and form a vacuum, because there's no oxygen left to hold that space. This is what keeps your jams, butters, and pickles fresh.

HOW TO PROCESS

1. If you're starting with brand-new jars, remove their lids and rings. If you're using older jars, check the rims to make sure there are no chips or cracks.

2. Put the rack into the canning pot and put the jars on top.

3. Fill the pot (and jars) with water to cover and bring to a boil. I have found that this is the very easiest way to heat up the jars in preparation for canning because you're going to have to heat up the canning pot anyway. Why not use that energy to heat up the jars as well?

4. Put the lids in a small saucepan, cover with water, and bring them to the barest simmer on the back of the stove.

5. While the canning pot comes to a boil, prepare your product.

6. When your recipe is complete, remove the jars from the canning pot (pouring the water back into the pot as you remove the jars) and set them on a clean towel on the counter. There's no need to invert them; the jars will be so hot that any remaining water will rapidly evaporate. Remove the lids from the saucepan with tongs or a magnetic lid wand and lay them out on the clean towel.

7. Carefully fill the jars with your product. Depending on the recipe, you'll need to leave between ¼ and ½ inch/6 and 12 mm of headspace (that's the room between the surface of the product and the top of the jar). Jams and jellies typically get ¼ inch/6 mm, while thicker products and pickles get ½ inch/12 mm.

8. Wipe the rims of the jar with a clean, damp paper towel or kitchen towel. If the product you're working with is very sticky, you can dip the edge of the cloth in distilled white vinegar for a bit of a cleaning boost.

9. Apply the lids and screw the bands on the jars to hold the lids down during processing. Tighten the bands with the tips of your fingers to ensure that they aren't overly tight. This is known as "fingertip tight."

10. Carefully lower the filled jars into the canning pot. You may need to remove some water as you put the jars in the pot, to keep it from over-flowing. A heat-resistant measuring cup is the best tool for this job. If you're canning in an asparagus or 4th burner pot, you will be stacking your jars. Take care as you do this.

11. Once the pot has returned to a rolling boil, start your timer. The length of the processing time will vary from recipe to recipe.

12. When your timer goes off, promptly remove the jars from the water bath. Gently place them back on the towel-lined countertop and let them cool.

13. The jar lids should begin to ping soon after they've been removed from the pot. The pinging is the sound of the seals forming; the center of the lids will become concave as the vacuum seal takes hold.

14. After the jars have cooled for 24 hours, remove the bands and check the seals. You do this by grasping the jar by the edges of the lid and gently lifting it an inch/2.5 cm or two off the countertop. The lid should hold fast.

15. Once you've determined that your seals are good, you can store your jars in a cool, dark place (with the rings off, please) for up to a year. Any jars with bad seals can still be used—just store them in the refrig-erator and use within 2 weeks.

HIGH ACID VS. LOW ACID

In the course of learning to can and then sharing my excitement about it, I've heard so many people confess their canning fears. Mostly, they're terrified that they are going to kill their families. Hear me now. If you stick to the high-acid foods—like most jams, jellies, and pickles—you are not going to kill anyone.

Botulism is the singular killer when it comes to canned goods, but it cannot grow in high-acid environments. This means that you'll never hear of a case of botulism having grown in a jar of strawberry jam or dill pickles. If something goes wrong with your high-acid foods, you will be able to tell immediately upon opening the jar. There will be a foul smell, colorful growth, or bubbling where there ought not be (and these things happen very rarely if you're following proper canning procedure).

There are a few varieties of fruit that exist in the very narrow gray area between high acid and low. These items need to acidified to be canned safely and should be treated with care. This list includes figs, white peaches, Asian pears, bananas, mangoes, all melon, and tomatoes. Take care when working with these fruits and always consult trusted recipe sources.

COOKING TIMES

In many of these recipes, I've included suggested cooking times. However, these are just ranges and are not ironclad, particularly when it comes to jams, jellies, and marmalades. Cooking times can vary depending on the humidity in the air, the moisture level in the fruit, the width of your pot, and the intensity of your stove's heat. It's important to use your judgment when cooking up these sweet preserves and not just depend solely on the suggested cooking times. Happily, these small batches cook up so quickly that it's easier to tell whether you've achieved a proper set.

TESTING FOR SET

There are a number of ways that you can test to ensure that your preserve is going to set. You can track its temperature with a candy or instant-read thermometer, as jams and jellies reach the set point at 220°F/105°C. You can run your spoon or spatula through cooking jam or jelly, hold it up over the pan, and watch how the drips fall. When a preserve is nearly done, wide-based droplets will cling firmly to the spatula. Or you can use the plate test. At the beginning of cooking time, put a couple of small plates or saucers into the freezer. When the preserve is nearly done, pull the pot off the stove, get one of your plates from the freezer, and place a small drop of the jam or jelly on the plate. Return it to the freezer for 2 minutes. When the time is up, remove the plate from the freezer and gently nudge the jam with the tip of your finger. If the surface wrinkles, that is a sign that your jam is done. If your finger runs right through it, the preserve needs a few more minutes on the stove.

YIELDS

Just like cooking times, the yields on these recipes can vary. I have tested and retested the recipes to ensure that they work, but there are so many factors that can nudge the final amount up or down a few ounces. One particular culprit is a rainy growing season. Lots of precipitation can cause fruits to take on more water while on the plant. This means that during cooking, there will be more liquid that has to be evaporated out of the fruit, leading to smaller yields. Conversely, during hotter, drier years, the fruit can become intense with sugar (this is why dry-farmed tomatoes and strawberries are so magically delicious) and can yield slightly more product. Unfortunately, it's all the more noticeable with these small batches if the yield is slightly off. I often compensate variable yields by adjusting the headspace a little. Even if a recipe calls for you to leave $1/2$ inch/12 mm of headspace, you can often get away with ¼ inch/6 mm or ¾ inch/2 cm, if that's what it takes to account for your yield.

SHELF LIFE

When it comes to storing your shelf-stable jams, pickles, and chutneys (anything that took a trip through the boiling water bath), know that they are best kept in a cool, dark place (direct sunlight is a particular enemy to home canned items). It's also best to remember that you've preserved this food for a time, not all time. Home-canned items are truly best eaten within a year of being made. Higher sugar preserves will often last a bit longer than that, but they too will eventually lose their quality.

ADJUSTING FOR ALTITUDE

One of the quirks of life on Earth is that as you increase your elevation, the temperature at which water boils decreases. With every reduction in degree, you lose a bit of bacteria-killing power. If you live between sea level and 1,000 feet/306 meters, you don't have to make any adjustments and can use the recipes as written. However, for additional altitude, you must add time to the processing step:

1,001 to 3,000 feet/ 306 to 915 meters, add 5 minutes
3,001 to 6,000 feet/ 916 to 1,830 meters, add 10 minutes
6,001 to 8,000 feet/ 1,831 to 2,440 meters, add 15 minutes
8,001 to 10,000 feet/ 2,441 to 3,050 meters, add 20 minutes

Spring
RECIPES

There is a year-round farmers' market just a couple of blocks from my apartment. I go to it nearly every Saturday morning to pick up eggs, honey, and whatever local, seasonal produce is available. In the summer and fall, the bounty is downright flamboyant, with tables piled high to overflowing with lettuces, zucchini, and peaches. Winter means pears, Brussels sprouts, and sturdy orange squash. The most meager time of year is very early spring. The storage apples are sad and good only for baking, and there are still weeks to go before the first stalks of asparagus arrive. It can be a challenge to keep up the weekly market visit when so little is new and truly fresh.

Still, I've found that even in the face of such slim pickings, there are still ingredients that beg to be preserved, if you look closely. Early radishes and snacking turnips make tasty pickles. Baby greens grown inside hoop houses can be whirled into verdant, restorative pestos.

Then, it's not long until the spring delicacies, such as ramps, fava beans, and garlic scapes arrive. Finally, the rhubarb and asparagus begin to push through the soil and the wild abundance of the growing season is upon us.

Fermented Radish Slices

Pickled Ramp Bulbs

Ramp Greens Kimchi

Pickled Spring Onions

Pickled Garlic Scape Segments

Garlic Scape and Arugula Pesto

Sorrel Pesto

Fava Bean, Parsley, and Walnut Pesto

Hakurei Turnip Quick Pickles

Spicy Mango Salsa

Spicy Pickled Asparagus

Marinated Sugar Snap Peas with Ginger and Mint

Quick Pickled Spring Peas

Marinated Lemon Cucumbers

Rosemary Rhubarb Jelly

Mustardy Rhubarb Chutney

Rhubarb and Meyer Lemon Marmalade

Oven-Roasted Rhubarb Compote

Whole Strawberries in Vanilla Syrup

Honey-Sweetened Strawberry Jam

Quick Pickled Strawberries

Mint-Lime Syrup

Fermented Radish Slices

R adishes are one of the first fresh vegetables out of the ground each spring and when you start spotting them, you know spring is really and truly coming. Because these pickles are never heated, they stay completely crisp. I like to tuck them into homemade banh mi sandwiches.

MAKES 1 (1-QUART/1-LITER) JAR

1 $\frac{1}{2}$ tablespoons finely milled sea salt
2 bunches fresh radishes (about 1 $\frac{1}{2}$ pounds/680g,
   including the greens)

Wash a wide-mouth 1-quart/1-liter jar and a quarter-pint/125 ml jar. In a small saucepan, bring 2 cups/480 ml of water to a boil. Once it boils vigorously, add the salt and remove the pot from the heat. Stir until the salt dissolves. Let the brine cool to room temperature.

Wash the radishes and trim away the roots and leaves. Thinly slice the radishes into disks $\frac{1}{4}$ inch/6 mm to $\frac{1}{2}$ inch/12 mm thick. Pack the radishes into the clean 1-quart/ 1-liter jar and cover with the cooled brine, leaving about an inch/2.5 cm of headspace.

Fit the quarter-pint/125 ml jar upright into the mouth of the 1-quart/1-liter jar. Pour the remaining brine into the quarter-pint/125 ml jar to weigh it down. Press the quarter-pint/125 ml jar down until the brine reaches the rim of the larger jar, so that the radishes are completely submerged.

Set the radish jar on a small plate or saucer to catch any drips of brine. Cover the jar with a small tea towel or a few layers of cheesecloth, and secure it with a rubber band. Let it sit on your counter for 5 to 7 days, until the brine goes slightly cloudy and the radishes taste quite tart. The edges of the radishes will bleed their color into the brine and the interior of the slices; don't be surprised by the change in color.

When they've reached the level of tang you like, remove the quarter-pint/125 ml jar, skim any scum from the top of the brine, place a lid on the 1-quart/1-liter jar, and refrigerate.

The fermented radishes will keep for several weeks in the refrigerator.

Note: Make sure that both jars are scrupulously clean. Because fermentation is a process of allowing beneficial bacteria to transform sugars into acid, you want to ensure that you've given the good bacteria unencumbered space in which to work.

Pickled Ramp Bulbs

There are few vegetables whose arrival is more eagerly anticipated each spring than that of the ramp. Part of its appeal is in its timing. It appears right at that moment when the over-wintered potatoes, apples, and squash have become soft, spotty, and entirely unappetizing. Ramps are green and fresh, tasting like a lusty cross between green onions and garlic. This particular pickle was heavily influenced by the basic pickling brine recipe in *The Wild Table*, an excellent book on foraged foods by Connie Green and Sarah Scott.

MAKES 1 (1-PINT/500 ML) JAR

1 pound/460 g ramps
$\frac{1}{2}$ cup/120 ml unseasoned rice vinegar
$\frac{1}{4}$ cup/50 g granulated sugar
1 teaspoon pickling salt (or any other finely milled salt)
$\frac{1}{2}$ teaspoon coriander seeds
$\frac{1}{2}$ teaspoon black peppercorns
$\frac{1}{8}$ teaspoon red chile flakes
1 bay leaf

Wash the ramps well. Trim away the leafy greens and root ends (see note).

Combine the vinegar, sugar, and salt with $\frac{1}{2}$ cup/120 ml of water in a small saucepan and bring to a boil.

Place all the spices and the bay leaf in the bottom of a clean 1-pint/500 ml jar and pack the trimmed ramps into the jar. Pour the brine over the ramps, leaving $\frac{1}{2}$ inch/12 mm of headspace. Tap the jar gently to remove any air bubbles. Add more liquid to return the headspace to $\frac{1}{2}$ inch/12 mm, if necessary. Wipe the rim and apply a clean lid and ring.

Let the jar cool for at least an hour and then place in the refrigerator. Give the ramps at least a week in the pickling liquid before eating.

Note: Because nothing about ramps is neat or precisely cultivated, you have to take a bit more care in their preparation. Wash them well in several changes of cold water to ensure you remove all the grit. And don't toss the green tops! You can either sauté them and serve them as a cooked green or whirl them into an oniony pesto. Or save them for Ramp Greens Kimchi (recipe follows).

Ramp Greens Kimchi

his recipe is inspired by a recipe posted in spring 2011 by the Hungry Tigress. She is one of my most beloved canning blog buddies and is always good for a dose of edible inspiration and illumination. This kimchi is funky, tangy, and delivers a giant wallop of flavor. I like to eat it with fried eggs, brown rice, and a little dab of sriracha.

MAKES 1 (HALF-PINT/250 ML) JAR

4 ounces (115 g) ramp greens
1 teaspoon finely milled sea salt
$\frac{1}{2}$ teaspoon granulated sugar
1 $\frac{1}{2}$ teaspoons Aleppo pepper
1 teaspoon minced fresh ginger
1 garlic clove, minced
$\frac{1}{2}$ teaspoon soy sauce
$\frac{1}{2}$ teaspoon toasted sesame oil

Clean the ramp greens well and shake them to remove the water. Collect the greens into a stack and chop into 1-inch/2.5 cm lengths. Place the ramp greens in a medium bowl and add the salt, sugar, Aleppo pepper, ginger, and garlic. Stir until well combined. Add the soy sauce and sesame oil and stir again.

Pack the seasoned ramp greens into a wide-mouth 1-pint/500 ml jar and loosely apply a lid. Let the jar rest at room temperature for 24 hours, then move it to the fridge.

Every day for the next 4 to 5 days, open the jar and stir the ramps with a clean spoon. The kimchi is done when its volume has reduced by half and it smells rich and savory. It will keep for up to a month in the fridge.

Pickled Spring Onions

O ne of my favorite springtime moments is when the new onions start appearing at the farmers' markets. While generally related to the storage onion we all know, these freshly pulled, uncured onions are smaller, sweeter, and more succulent than their elderly brethren. They typically still have their green shoots attached, which are also entirely edible. Much like their cousin, the ramp, they let off a musky scent if placed in your refrigerator unwrapped. Once pickled, they are endlessly useful. Try them on a burger, on top of goat cheese toasts, or tossed into a salad of young arugula and toasted walnuts.

MAKES 2 (HALF-PINT/250 ML) JARS

1 bunch spring onions (about 8 ounces/
   225 g once trimmed and cleaned)
$\frac{1}{2}$ cup/120 ml cider vinegar
3 tablespoons granulated sugar
1 teaspoon finely milled sea salt
1 teaspoon yellow mustard seeds
$\frac{1}{2}$ teaspoon celery seeds
$\frac{1}{8}$ teaspoon red chile flakes

Prepare a small boiling water bath and 2 half-pint/250 ml jars according to the process on page 11. Place 2 lids in a small saucepan of water and bring to a gentle simmer.

Wash and thinly slice the trimmed spring onions into rounds. In a small saucepan, combine the vinegar, $\frac{1}{2}$ cup/120 ml of water, sugar, salt, mustard seeds, celery seeds, and chile flakes. Bring to a boil and add the onions.

Stir to combine and cook for 2 to 3 minutes, until the onions are heated through. Remove the pot from the heat and funnel the onions into the prepared jars. Wipe the rims, apply the lids and rings, and process in a boiling water bath for 10 minutes (see pages 11–12).

Pickled Garlic Scape Segments

arlic scapes are the green curly shoots that grow from hard-neck garlic plants in early spring. Farmers remove them so that garlic plants will concentrate their growth energy into the bulbs. Once considered farm leavings, in recent years they've become one of the most popular farmers' market items in April and May. They have a gentle garlic flavor and make an excellent pickle that ends up tasting like a crisp, garlicky dilly bean.

MAKES 2 (HALF-PINT/250 ML) JARS

8 ounces/225 g garlic scapes (2 to 3 bunches)
$^3/_4$ cup/180 ml cider vinegar
1 tablespoon pickling salt
1 teaspoon dill seeds
$^1/_2$ teaspoon black peppercorns
$^1/_2$ teaspoon red chile flakes

Prepare a boiling water bath and 2 half-pint/250 ml jars according to the process on page 11. Place 2 lids in a small saucepan of water and bring to a gentle simmer.

Combine the vinegar, $^3/_4$ cup/180 ml of water, and the pickling salt in a medium pot and bring to a boil.

Trim the ends of the scapes, and cut them into segments about 2 inches/5 cm in length.

Add the scape segments to the pot of brine and stir for 30 seconds. Remove the pot from heat. Divide the spices evenly between the prepared jars and funnel in the warmed scape segments on top of them. Ladle the brine over the scapes, leaving $^1/_2$ inch/12 mm of headspace. Tap the jars gently to remove any air bubbles. Add more liquid to return the headspace to $^1/_2$ inch/12 mm, if necessary. Wipe the rims, apply the lids and rings, and process in a boiling water bath for 10 minutes (see pages 11–12). Let these pickles cure for at least a week before eating.

Note: You won't typically find garlic scapes in your local grocery store. They tend to be a farmers' market, natural food store, or CSA-only item. If you struggle to get some, make sure to ask at a local market: chances are good that a farmer will bring some in for you.

Garlic Scape and Arugula Pesto

I n early spring, baby greens and garlic scapes are among some of the first new produce to appear at farmers' markets. My favorite of those young greens is arugula, because it has a bright, peppery bite. It also pairs up perfectly with garlic scapes. This pesto marries the gentle garlic flavor of the scapes with the sharpness of arugula. It's great on pasta or stirred into a warm salad of quinoa and roasted vegetables.

MAKES 1 (HALF-PINT/250 ML) JAR

8 ounces/225 g garlic scapes (2 to 3 bunches)
1 cup/20 g packed arugula leaves
$\frac{1}{2}$ cup/70 g pine nuts, toasted
$\frac{1}{4}$ cup/25 g grated Parmesan cheese
$\frac{1}{4}$ cup/60 ml olive oil, plus more as needed
Salt and freshly ground black pepper

Chop the garlic scapes into 1-inch/2.5 cm lengths and combine them with the arugula leaves, toasted pine nuts, and Parmesan cheese in the bowl of a food processor. Pulse until a paste begins to form. Remove the lid and scrape down the bowl, if necessary.

Once you've gotten to a chunky paste, slowly stream in the $\frac{1}{4}$ cup/60 ml of olive oil with the motor running and process until well combined. Taste and adjust the seasoning to taste.

Pack the pesto into a half-pint/250 ml jar (if you're freezing it, try dividing it between 2 quarter-pint/125 ml jars). Cover with a thin layer of olive oil (it keeps out the oxygen and prevents the top of the pesto from browning) and either refrigerate or freeze. It will keep in the refrigerator for at least a week, or in the freezer for up to a year.

Sorrel Pesto

orrel is a green that grows wild in the spring and early summer. There are several varieties, but the most common variety looks like a pointy spinach leaf or squat clover. It tastes tart and fresh and makes a wonderfully verdant pesto. I have a friend with a small patch in a community garden, where pointy-leafed sorrel grows wild between the plots. She brings me heaps and oodles of it during its season. I particularly love eating it with grilled salmon fillets and boiled new potatoes.

MAKES 1 (HALF-PINT/250 ML) JAR

2 cups/450 g packed clean sorrel leaves
$\frac{1}{2}$ cup/27.5 g blanched and slivered almonds, toasted
2 garlic cloves
$\frac{1}{2}$ teaspoon finely milled sea salt
$\frac{1}{4}$ teaspoon freshly ground black pepper
$\frac{1}{4}$ cup/60 ml olive oil, plus more as needed

Roughly chop the sorrel leaves and combine them with the almonds, garlic, salt, and pepper in the bowl of a food processor. Pulse until a paste begins to form. Remove the lid and scrape down the bowl, if necessary. Once you've gotten to a chunky paste, slowly stream in the $\frac{1}{4}$ cup/60 ml of olive oil with the motor running and process until well combined. Taste and adjust the seasoning.

Pack the pesto into a half-pint/250 ml jar (if you're freezing it, try dividing it between two quarter-pint/125 ml jars). Cover with a thin layer of olive oil (it keeps out the oxygen and prevents the top of the pesto from browning) and either refrigerate or freeze. It will keep in the refrigerator for at least a week, or in the freezer for up to a year.

Fava Bean, Parsley, and Walnut Pesto

I make a lot of pesto in the spring and fall, when plenty of good, flavorful greens and herbs are available. I toss them with pasta, use them to dress grain salads, and dollop them on meat and fish for extra flavor. I always have a couple of different varieties of pesto in my freezer at any given time and I consider them one of my very best pantry tools. This version is particularly good smeared onto sourdough toasts with some fresh ricotta cheese.

MAKES 1 (1-PINT/500 ML) JAR

1 pound/460 g fresh fava beans in their pods
Leaves from 2 bunches flat-leaf parsley
2 garlic cloves
Juice of $\frac{1}{2}$ lemon
1 cup/100 g walnuts halves, toasted and cooled
$\frac{1}{2}$ cup/60 g freshly grated aged pecorino cheese
$\frac{1}{2}$ teaspoon finely milled sea salt, plus more as needed
$\frac{1}{2}$ cup/120 ml walnut oil, plus more as needed

Bring a pot of salted water to a boil. While the water heats, remove the fava beans from their long pods. Once the water boils, add the fava beans and cook until bright green and just tender, about 3 minutes. Drain and immediately rinse under cold water. Pop the bright green fava beans out of their skins and set aside.

In the bowl of a food processor, combine the parsley leaves, garlic, lemon juice, walnuts, cheese, salt, and peeled fava beans. Pulse until the mixture becomes a chunky paste, removing the lid and scraping down the sides of the bowl when necessary.

Once you've gotten to a chunky paste, slowly stream in the $\frac{1}{2}$ cup/120 ml of walnut oil with the motor running and process until well combined. Taste and adjust the seasoning.

Pack the pesto into a half-pint jar (if you're freezing it, try dividing it between 2 quarter-pint/125 ml jars). Cover with a thin layer of walnut oil (it keeps out the oxygen and prevents the top of the pesto from browning) and either refrigerate or freeze. It will keep in the refrigerator for at least a week, or in the freezer for up to a year.

Hakurei Turnip Quick Pickles

The first time I saw a Hakurei turnip, I thought I was looking at a strain of albino radish. It was at a farmers' market, back in my very early days as a local eater and pickler. I asked the farmer and he explained that they're a Japanese strain of turnip sown in early spring, and they're ready to harvest in just a month. Thus began my love affair with this young, creamy-fleshed root. Each spring, I look forward to their arrival at the market. They have a texture similar to that of radishes, but without the latter's signature pepperiness. They are good eaten raw or in this quick, tasty pickle.

MAKES 1 (1-PINT/500 ML) JAR

2 bunches Hakurei turnips (about 1 pound/460 g)
2 teaspoons finely milled sea salt
1 cup/250 ml unseasoned rice vinegar
1 tablespoon granulated sugar
$1/2$ teaspoon black peppercorns, crushed
3 slices fresh ginger

Wash the turnips well and slice them thinly on a mandoline. Place the slices in a small bowl and toss with the salt. Let them rest for at least an hour, until they produce liquid.

While the salted turnips rest, combine the vinegar, sugar, peppercorns, and ginger in a small saucepan and heat until the sugar is dissolved.

Drain the turnip slices and pack them into a 1-pint/500 ml jar.

Pour the brine over the turnip slices, leaving $1/2$ inch/25mm. Tap the jar gently to remove any air bubbles. Add more liquid to return the headspace to $1/2$ inch/25mm, if necessary. Place a lid on the jar, let the turnips cool to room temperature, and refrigerate. The turnips will keep for at least a week in the fridge.

Note: A useful thing about Hakurei turnips is that their greens are just as tasty as their roots. You can eat them raw, wilt them into a sauté, or purée them with a head of green garlic, toasted nuts, and olive oil into an impressively vivid pesto.

Spicy Mango Salsa

angoes don't grow anywhere near my home in Philadelphia, but every spring there is a week when a mountain of them appears in the entrance to my local Whole Foods Market. During their season, I buy a few every time I grocery shop. I love them diced on yogurt or slivered into salads. This salsa is one of the ways that I preserve them when I've finally eaten my fill.

MAKES 3 (HALF-PINT/250 ML) JARS

2 to 3 slightly underripe Ataulfo mangoes, peeled, seeded, and chopped (about 2 cups/350 g)

$^3/_4$ cup/115 g seeded and chopped red bell pepper

$^3/_4$ cup/180 ml cider vinegar

$^1/_2$ cup/115 g packed light brown sugar

$^1/_4$ cup/40 g minced shallot

1 tablespoon grated fresh ginger

1 teaspoon Aleppo pepper

$^1/_4$ teaspoon cayenne pepper

Prepare a boiling water bath and 3 half-pint/250 ml jars according to the process on page 11. Place 3 canning lids in a small saucepan of water and bring to a gentle simmer.

Combine all the salsa ingredients in a large pot over high heat and bring to a boil. Lower the heat to medium and let the salsa simmer for just 3 to 5 minutes, until it no longer looks watery.

When the salsa is finished cooking, funnel it into the prepared jars, leaving $^1/_2$ inch/12mm of headspace. Tap the jars gently to remove any air bubbles. Add more liquid to return the headspace to $^1/_2$ inch/12 mm, if necessary. Wipe the rims, apply the lids and bands, and process in a boiling water bath for 10 minutes (see pages 11–12).

Spicy Pickled Asparagus

I went to college in a town surrounded by asparagus fields. Every spring, roadside stands would spring up, selling it for 69 cents a pound. I'd eat bundle after bundle, in the hopes of getting my fill for the year. If only I'd known then that those bright green spears made a perfect pickle! I often eat them for lunch, wrapped up in a slice of smoked turkey.

MAKES 2 (12-OUNCE/360 ML) JARS

1 pound/460 g thin asparagus spears,
  trimmed to fit your jars

1 cup/240 ml cider vinegar

1 tablespoon pickling salt

4 garlic cloves, peeled

2 teaspoons crushed red chile flakes

$\frac{1}{2}$ teaspoon cayenne pepper

Prepare a boiling water bath and 2 (12-ounce/360 ml) jelly jars according to the process on page 11. Place 2 lids in a small saucepan of water and bring to a gentle simmer.

Combine the vinegar, 1 cup/240 ml of water, and the salt in a separate small saucepan and bring to a boil.

Fill a pan with 4 inches/10 cm of water and bring to a boil to blanch the asparagus. While the water heats, wash the asparagus and trim off the bottoms to fit the stalks into your jars.

When the water is boiling, blanch the asparagus for 60 seconds. When the time is up, transfer the asparagus to a colander and rinse with cold water.

Divide the garlic cloves, chile flakes, and cayenne evenly between the jars. Pack the asparagus spears into the prepared jars. Pour the pickling liquid over the asparagus, leaving $\frac{1}{2}$ inch/12 mm of headspace. Tap the jars gently to remove any air bubbles. Add more liquid to return the headspace to $\frac{1}{2}$ inch/12 mm, if necessary. Wipe the rims, apply the lids and rings, and process the jars in a boiling water bath for 10 minutes (see pages 11–12). Let the asparagus cure for at least a week before eating.

Marinated Sugar Snap Peas with Ginger and Mint

Although I like them raw or gently sautéed until tender-crisp, one of my favorite things to do to sugar snap peas is to quickly pickle them in a gingery, barely sweetened brine. I make them as a refrigerator pickle so that they retain their crunch and regularly eat them with open-face sandwiches or chopped and tossed with grain salads.

MAKES 1 (1-QUART/1-LITER) JAR

1½ cups/360 ml unseasoned rice vinegar

1 tablespoon honey

1 teaspoon finely milled sea salt

1 pound/460 g sugar snap peas

1 green onion

1 sprig fresh mint

3 thin slices fresh ginger

In a small saucepan, combine the vinegar, honey, and salt. Heat until the honey and salt are entirely dissolved.

Wash the sugar snap peas well. Using a knife, trim both ends and remove the tough string that runs along the back of the peas. Cut the green onion into 2 or 3 segments, so that they fit the jar. Stand them up in a clean 1-quart/1-liter jar, along with the mint sprig and the ginger slices.

Pack the prepared sugar snaps into the jar. If they don't all fit, set them aside. You may be able to sneak them in once the pickling liquid is poured.

Pour the hot vinegar mixture over the sugar snaps. Tap the jar gently on the counter to remove any air bubbles. If you had any remaining peas, try to pack them into the jar at this time.

Place a lid on the jar and let the jar rest until it has cooled to room temperature. Refrigerate. Let these pickles sit in the vinegar for at least 24 hours before eating. They will keep for up to a week in the refrigerator.

Note: Make sure to use the freshest sugar snap peas you can find. No pickling brine can restore crunch to a pea that's lost it to age. If you can't find sugar snaps, this recipe works equally well with crisp snow peas.

Quick Pickled Spring Peas

Fresh peas are one of the true edible embodiments of spring. There is nothing better than a few tender green orbs, eaten straight from the pod. However, they are not without their issues. They're both labor intensive and expensive (if you're not growing them yourself), and their season is so fleeting. As a preserver, I'm always looking for ways to extend short seasons and make precious ingredients stretch, so I worked my pickling mojo on spring peas. The result of my efforts is this pickled pea, which manages to layer both the essence of pea flavor with the energetic pungency of vinegar. I like to toss them into salads, or stir them into risotto at the end of cooking.

MAKES 1 (1-PINT/500 ML) JAR

1 tablespoon olive oil
1½ cups/225 g shelled peas
½ teaspoon finely milled sea salt
2 tablespoons granulated sugar
¼ cup/60 ml sherry vinegar
1 garlic clove, roughly chopped
1 tablespoon torn fresh mint leaves

Heat the oil in a large skillet over medium-high heat. When it shimmers, add the peas and cook them for 2 to 3 minutes, until they soften and lose their raw taste.

Add the salt and sugar and swirl the pan so that they dissolve.

Remove the pan from the heat and pour in the vinegar. (It should steam and sputter; try to avoid breathing in the steam.) Add the garlic and mint and toss to incorporate. Funnel the peas, mint, and brine into a 1-pint/500 ml jar.

Once the jar is cool, apply a lid, place the peas in the refrigerator, and let them rest for 12 to 24 hours.

The pickled peas will keep for up to 1 week in the refrigerator.

Note: Make sure you're working with the freshest peas you can get. If you're shopping at the farmers' market, make this pickle the same day you buy so that the peas don't turn into little starch bombs.

Marinated Lemon Cucumbers

rom their name, you might assume that lemon cucumbers have a tart or acidic flavor. However, as soon as you catch sight of your first one, you'll see that they look like nothing so much as small, spiky lemons. And when you cut one in half, you'll see that it is cucumber through and through. I peel them, remove their seeds and cover them in vinaigrette. Because this is essentially a quick pickle, they're ready to eat within an hour of prep, but also keep well in the fridge for up to a week. I like to pack them into half-pint/250 ml jars and eat them as a little side salad with my lunch. They can be a refreshing nibble alongside drinks at a party, or as a condiment at a cookout.

MAKES 3 (HALF-PINT/250 ML) JARS

1 pint lemon cucumbers, peeled, seeded, and cut into chunks
(about 12 ounces/350 g)
$\frac{1}{2}$ cup/120 ml red wine vinegar
$\frac{1}{4}$ cup/60 ml olive oil
3 tablespoons minced red onion
1 garlic clove, minced
1 tablespoon granulated sugar
1 teaspoon dried dill
1 teaspoon finely milled sea salt
5 to 6 grinds black pepper

Divide the prepared cucumbers among 3 half-pint/250 ml jars. Whisk together the vinegar, olive oil, red onion, garlic, sugar, dill, salt, and pepper. Divide the vinaigrette evenly among the jars of cucumbers. Wipe the rims, apply the lids and rings firmly, and give each jar a good shake.

Let the cucumbers marinate for at least an hour before serving. They will keep in the fridge for up to a week.

Brunch

My maternal grandmother was known among her friends for her ability to throw an excellent party. She always had a generously stocked bar, served plenty of good cheese and crackers to go with drinks, and never failed to follow cocktail hour with a glorious spread of food. If you happened to ask for her secret to dinner party success, she'd happily tell you. She employed a very skilled caterer.

When I was twenty-three years old, I inherited my grandmother's apartment, complete with her extensive collection of stemware, serving platters, and silver for twenty-four. The only thing I didn't inherit was the funds necessary to hire the caterer.

However, it seemed a great waste not employ all these party accessories. I began casting about for a way to have my friends over that wouldn't break me financially but would still make good use of the two dozen fine porcelain coffee cups I now owned.

And so, I started throwing brunch parties. In the beginning, my brunches were fairly spare. I'd make a big pan of scrambled eggs, use the oven to cook a pound of bacon until crisp, and pick up a dozen bagels. Friends would be assigned to bring orange juice and Champagne and we'd be all set.

However, it all changed when I became a canner. I started planning brunches entirely around the contents of my pantry. These days, when I invite friends over for brunch, they know that they're going to be treated to a jam bar.

I pull out all the open jam in my fridge (it's always a considerable amount). I buy a big container of Greek yogurt, toast up a pan of homemade granola, and make a double batch of whole wheat biscuits. I put out an assortment of silverware, plates, and bowls and invite my guests to go to town.

Some people build their own granola, jam, and yogurt parfaits. Others butter and jam their biscuits until content. For those who must have something savory, I scramble eggs, brown sausage patties, and set up station for DIY breakfast sandwiches (they are particularly good with a little tomato jam).

We sit, we drink coffee, and we eat until the biscuits are gone.

Whole Wheat Biscuits

MAKES 6 BISCUITS

1 cup/130 g whole wheat pastry flour
1$\frac{1}{2}$ teaspoons baking powder
$\frac{1}{2}$ teaspoon finely milled sea salt
1 tablespoon granulated sugar
3 tablespoons cold unsalted butter
$\frac{1}{3}$ cup/80ml cold buttermilk

Preheat the oven to 425°F/220°C. Sift the dry ingredients together. Using a pastry blender, cut the butter into the flour mixture until it is pebbly. Add the buttermilk and stir until the dough just comes together.

Turn out the dough onto a clean board or countertop. Knead for 30 seconds and then pat out the dough to about 1 inch/2.5 cm thick. Using a clean glass or biscuit cutter about 2$\frac{1}{2}$ inches/6.3 cm in diameter, cut the dough into rounds.

Lay the cut biscuits an inch/2.5 cm apart on an ungreased baking sheet and bake for 10 to 12 minutes, until the tops are brown and the biscuits have puffed up tall.

Remove from the oven and serve warm.

Rosemary Rhubarb Jelly

here is something about the combination of rhubarb and rosemary that speaks to me. The bright, apple-y flavor of rhubarb just seems to call out for the woodsy, herbaceousness of rosemary and I am always happy to help them come together. This pretty jelly is entirely magical when eaten with fresh spring cheeses.

MAKES 3 (HALF-PINT/250 ML) JARS

1 pound/460 g bright red rhubarb, chopped
2 large sprigs rosemary, divided
1½ cups granulated sugar
1 tablespoon powdered pectin

Combine the rhubarb, 1 large rosemary sprig, and 1½ cups/360 ml of water in a large pot, cover, and simmer together over medium-high heat for 20 to 25 minutes. Cook until the rhubarb has completely broken down and the water is tinted a vivid pink.

Line a fine-mesh sieve with cheesecloth and place it over a large bowl. Pour the cooked rhubarb through it. Let the sieve sit and drip for at least half an hour. Do not press the rhubarb pulp, as that will make your jelly cloudy. When the rhubarb juice is finished dripping through the sieve, discard the solids and measure out 2 cups/475 ml of rhubarb juice.

Prepare a boiling water bath and 3 half-pint/250 ml jars according to the process on page 11. Place 3 lids in a small saucepan of water and bring to a gentle simmer. Tuck 2 saucers into the freezer to use at the end of cooking to test the set.

Measure the sugar and whisk in the pectin thoroughly.

In a large, nonreactive pot, combine the rhubarb juice and the pectin-spiked sugar. Once the sugar is dissolved, taste the rhubarb juice to gauge the rosemary flavor. If you like it as it is, proceed with cooking. If not, add the remaining rosemary sprig.

Bring to a boil and cook, stirring frequently, until the volume in the pot is greatly reduced.

While you continue to stir, clip a candy thermometer to the pot and watch until the pot reaches 220°F/105°C. There will be a great deal of foaming and bubbling before it reaches this point. It should look thick and syrupy and the bubbles should look glossy. Use the frozen saucer to test doneness.

When the jelly is finished cooking, pour it into the prepared jars. If you added additional rosemary, remove it at this time. Wipe the rims, apply the lids and bands, and process in a boiling water bath for 10 minutes (see pages 11–12).

Mustardy Rhubarb Chutney

I f the idea of homemade condiments has you a little intimidated, chutney makes for a very good starting place. Once your fruits and vegetables are chopped, you simply toss them in a wide, nonreactive pan and cook. This small batch takes about 45 minutes over medium heat to cook down into a thick, slightly sticky, spreadable condiment. Paired with a log of goat cheese and a packet of good crackers, it's my go-to contribution to casual parties and potlucks.

MAKES 3 (HALF-PINT/250 ML) JARS

1 pound/460 g rhubarb, chopped into $\frac{1}{2}$-inch/12 mm pieces
1 small yellow onion, minced
$\frac{3}{4}$ cup/115 g dried currants
$1\frac{1}{2}$ cups/340 g packed dark brown sugar
$1\frac{1}{2}$ cups/360 ml cider vinegar
3 teaspoons yellow mustard seeds
2 teaspoons finely milled sea salt
1 teaspoon ground cinnamon
1 teaspoons grated fresh ginger
$\frac{1}{4}$ teaspoon Aleppo pepper

Prepare a boiling water bath and 3 half-pint/250 ml jars according to the process on page 11. Place 3 lids in a small saucepan of water and bring to a gentle simmer.

Combine all the ingredients in a wide, nonreactive pan, place it over high heat, and bring it to a boil. Once it bubbles, lower the heat to medium and simmer gently, stirring regularly, until slightly thickened.

As the chutney gets closer to done, make sure to stir every minute or so to prevent scorching. You'll know the chutney is finished cooking when you can pull your spoon through the chutney and the space you've created doesn't fill in immediately.

Funnel the chutney into the prepared jars. Wipe the rims, apply the lids and rings, and process in a boiling water bath for 10 minutes (see pages 11–12).

Note: Another good way to determine whether the chutney is done is a method popular in vintage canning books. You scoop a small spoonful out of the pot and watch how it behaves in the bowl of the spoon. If it runs to the edges, it's not there yet. However, if it sits in a high mound, it is done.

Rhubarb and Meyer Lemon Marmalade

I f you're a marmalade lover and looking for a new variation, this is a wonderful combination of sweet and tart. It's so good in a batch of homemade lemon chicken, or used to fill thumbprint cookies.

MAKES 4 (HALF-PINT/250 ML) JARS

1 pound/355 g thin-skinned Meyer lemons
3 cups/600 g granulated sugar
8 ounces/225 g red rhubarb, cut into fine slices

Wash the lemons in warm, soapy water and dry thoroughly. Using a very sharp knife, cut both the flower and stem ends off the fruit. Sit each trimmed lemon on one of its newly flat ends and cut it into 6 wedges. Lay each wedge on its side and cut away the strip of inner membrane and the seeds. Reserve the trimmed pith and seeds (we'll be using them as a pectin source).

Thinly slice each trimmed wedge. What you want to end up with are bits of lemon that are no more than 1/4 inch/6 mm thick (1/8 inch/3 mm thick is even better) and no more than 1 1/2 inches/4 cm in length. Repeat this with all the lemons.

Place the lemon confetti in a bowl and cover with 2 cups/475 ml of water. Bundle up the reserved seeds and inner membranes into a length of cheesecloth, tie the ends tightly, and pop that into the bowl. Cover and place it in the refrigerator overnight (it can be left this way for up to 48 hours, which is good for those of us who lead busy lives).

Prepare a boiling water bath and 4 half-pint/250 ml jars according to the process on page 11. Place 4 lids in a small saucepan of water and bring to a gentle simmer.

Pour the lemons, pectin bundle, and water in a large pot. Add the sugar and stir to dissolve. Place the pot over high heat, bring to a boil, and cook for 15 to 25 minutes, until it reaches 220°F/105°C. In the last few minutes of cooking, stir in the rhubarb bits. Once it has reached temperature and seems quite thick, remove the marmalade from the heat. Funnel into the prepared jars, leaving 1/2 inch/12 mm of headspace. Wipe the rims, apply the lids and rings, and process in a boiling water bath for 10 minutes (see pages 11–12).

Oven-Roasted Rhubarb Compote

Part of the pleasure of rhubarb is its natural tartness. This recipe uses the minimum sugar necessary to tame that pucker without overrunning it entirely. I've been known to open a half-pint/250 ml jar of this compote, pour in a generous scoop of granola, and call it instant cobbler. Dessert is served!

MAKES 2 (HALF-PINT/250 ML) JARS

1 pound/355 g rhubarb
$\frac{1}{4}$ cup/50 g granulated sugar
2 vanilla beans
1 lemon

Preheat the oven to 350°F/180°C.

Wash the rhubarb and chop into 2-inch/5 cm lengths. Arrange the rhubarb pieces in the bottom of an oven-safe baking dish.

Put the sugar in a small mixing bowl. Scrape the vanilla bean seeds from the pods and add it to the sugar. Using a fine rasp, grate the lemon zest into the sugar. Toss the sugar, vanilla seeds, and lemon zest together and sprinkle over the rhubarb pieces. Cut the lemon in half and squeeze the juice from one half over the rhubarb.

Place the baking dish in the preheated oven and roast for 20 to 25 minutes, until the rhubarb pieces are quite tender but have not lost their shape. When they're done, their color will have faded into a dusky pink.

While the rhubarb roasts, prepare a boiling water bath and 2 half-pint/250 ml jars according to the process on page 11. Place 2 lids in a small saucepan of water and bring to a gentle simmer.

Scoop the roasted rhubarb into the prepared jars. Wipe the rims, apply the lids and rings, and process in a boiling water bath for 10 minutes (see pages 11–12).

Whole Strawberries in Vanilla Syrup

These preserved strawberries are a bit fussier than my normal slapdash approach to fruit, but they are well worth the effort. It's particularly important that you give them time to rest after cooking, as this leads to the best finished texture. Spoon these strawberries into plain yogurt or eat them with pound cake. I have the classic canning bible, *So Easy to Preserve*, to thank for this preserving technique.

MAKES 3 (HALF-PINT/250 ML) JARS

1 dry quart small, ripe strawberries (about $1\frac{1}{2}$ pounds/680 g)
$3\frac{1}{2}$ cups/700 g granulated sugar
1 vanilla bean, split and scraped
$\frac{1}{4}$ cup/60 ml freshly squeezed lemon juice

Wash the berries and remove the stems and leaves. Place the berries in a medium bowl and cover them with the sugar. Add the vanilla seeds and bean and stir gently to combine. Cover the bowl and refrigerate it for 2 to 3 hours.

When the time is up, carefully pour the strawberries, vanilla bean, juices, and any remaining sugar into a shallow, wide pan. Add the lemon juice and slowly bring to a boil. Cook the berries at a boil for 10 to 12 minutes, until they go a bit translucent and their syrup is thick.

Pour the berries and syrup into a shallow bowl, cool, and refrigerate, uncovered, for a day, jiggling the bowl occasionally to help distribute the strawberries in the syrup.

When you're ready to can, prepare a boiling water bath and 3 half-pint/250 ml jars according to the process on page 11. Place 3 lids in a small saucepan of water and bring to a gentle simmer. Scrape the strawberry mixture into a medium pan and heat to a simmer. Ladle the berries into the prepared jars and cover with the syrup, leaving $\frac{1}{2}$ inch/12 mm of headspace. Tap the jars gently to remove any air bubbles. Add more liquid to return the headspace to $\frac{1}{2}$ inch/12 mm, if necessary. Wipe the rims, apply the lids and rings, and process in a boiling water bath for 10 minutes (see pages 11–12).

Note: Because these berries need to sit uncovered in your fridge for a day, make sure that nothing with a particularly strong smell is sharing your refrigerator during the same 24-hour time period.

Honey-Sweetened Strawberry Jam

few years ago, I attended a party at which the dessert was an enormous tray of ripe, local strawberries. The berries were artfully arranged around a jar of honey from nearby hives. And though the berries were plenty sweet all on their own, our host encouraged us to dip them in the honey before taking a bite. The combination of strawberries and honey was a revelation and within minutes, I was imagining this jam. It's something I make at least once a week during strawberry season so I can squirrel away enough to keep me satisfied for the year to come.

MAKES 2 (HALF-PINT/250 ML) JARS

1 dry quart strawberries (about 1 ½ pounds/680 g)
1 cup/340 g honey
5 to 6 sprigs thyme
Juice of ½ lemon

Prepare a boiling water bath and 2 half-pint/250 ml jars according to the process on page 11. Place 2 lids in a small saucepan of water and bring to a gentle simmer.

Hull and chop the berries and place them in a bowl. Add the honey and stir. Strip the thyme leaves off their stems and add them to the strawberries and honey. Stir to combine and let sit for at least 10 minutes.

When the honey has dissolved and the strawberries are quite juicy, scrape the mixture into a wide pan. Bring to a bubble and cook over high heat for 8 to 12 minutes, stirring regularly, until the jam is thick and sticky. It is done when you can pull a spatula through the cooking fruit and it doesn't immediately rush in to fill the space.

Funnel the jam into the prepared jars. Wipe the rims, apply the lids and rings, and process in a boiling water bath for 10 minutes (see pages 11–12).

Notes: Once opened, preserves sweetened with honey don't last as long as those made with sugar. If your household can't eat a half-pint/250 ml jar of this jam within 2 or 3 weeks, consider canning it in quarter-pint/125 ml jars.

Quick Pickled Strawberries

I am a fool for any sweet and tangy combination of fruit, vinegar, and flavorful aromatics. In deep summer, I pickle peaches. In fall, pears get the tangy treatment. Cranberries happen in winter and in early spring, I always pickle some of those perfect, totally red local strawberries that you can only find at farmers' markets and U-pick farms. Because they're so fragile, I try to get them into the brine as soon as I get home from the market. Try them over young salad greens or added to a glass of sparkling water.

MAKES 1 SCANT (1-QUART/1-LITER) JAR

1 dry quart strawberries (about 1 $\frac{1}{2}$ pounds/680 g)
$\frac{3}{4}$ cup/180 ml Champagne vinegar
1 tablespoon granulated sugar
1 tablespoon finely milled sea salt
1 teaspoon cracked black peppercorns
2 sprigs tarragon

Wash the strawberries, remove the stems and leaves, and cut into halves or quarters, depending on their size.

In a medium saucepan, combine the vinegar with $\frac{1}{3}$ cup/80 ml of water, the sugar, salt, and peppercorns. Set over high heat and bring to a boil.

Place the tarragon in a wide-mouth 1-quart/1-liter jar and add the chopped berries. Once the brine has boiled, pour it over the strawberries. Let the pickles cool until room temperature, and then place a lid on the jar and refrigerate.

Allow these pickles to rest for at least 24 hours before eating.

Mint-Lime Syrup

Friends of mine have a garden with the most energetic mint plant I've ever seen. It is enthusiastic, intensely minty, and seems to thrive on being trimmed. Whenever I visit their house during the summer, they insist I help tame this plant and take home a giant bag of mint. I dry some, make fresh mint tea, and finally, cook up a batch of this syrup. It is minty heaven.

MAKES 1 (1-PINT/500 ML) JAR

2 cups/400 g granulated sugar
2 cups/80 g packed mint leaves, washed
Juice of 2 limes

Combine the sugar with 1 cup/250 ml of water in a medium saucepan. Place over medium-high heat and stir until the sugar dissolves. Add the mint leaves and lime juice and stir to combine. Simmer for 5 to 6 minutes, stirring regularly. Remove the pot from the heat and allow it to sit until cool.

Strain the mint out of the syrup and pour into a 1-pint/500 ml jar. Place a lid on the jar and pop it into the fridge. It will keep for weeks in the fridge.

Summer
RECIPES

Summer is the high season for food preservers. Farmers' markets overflow with stone fruit, herbs, and cucumbers of all shapes and sizes. Growers order larger boxes in which to pack their CSA shares. And backyard gardens belch forth zucchini, tomatoes, and eggplant like you've never seen before. There is just so gosh darn much available that it's easy to get overwhelmed by the abundance and decide to sit out the canning season entirely. Happily, that's where these micro batch recipes come in. Instead of being overwhelmed by the seasonal bounty, start small. A dry quart of cucumbers will make two crisp, puckery jars of pickles. One pound of plums can make enough jam for you and a friend. And that wild patch of herbs in your backyard? Gather them, give them a rough chop, and pack them with salt. They'll deliver flavor to soups and stews for the next year.

Honey-Sweetened Apricot Lavender Butter

Apricot Rosemary Jam

Apricot Almond Conserve

Sweet Cherry Compote

Sour Cherries with Bourbon

Salted Brown Sugar Peach Jam

Peach Jam with Sriracha

Peach Barbecue Sauce

Pickled Nectarine Slices

Nectarine Jam with Lemon Verbena and Honey

Blueberry Jam with Crystallized Ginger

Blueberry Maple Jam

Pickled Wax Beans

Garlic Dill Pickle Spears

Black Plum Chutney

Italian Plum Jam with Star Anise

Yellow Plum Jam with Vanilla

Raspberry Habanero Jam

Black Raspberry Preserves

Seedy Spiced Blackberry Jam

Preserved Fig Quarters with Whiskey

Marinated Red Peppers

Bread-and-Butter Zucchini Pickles

Zucchini Butter with Fresh Thyme

Salt-Preserved Herbs

Thai Basil Pesto

Orange Tomato and Smoked Paprika Jam

Blender Salsa

Slow-Roasted Grape Tomato Spread

Corn and Tomato Relish

Honey-Sweetened Apricot Lavender Butter

As a canner, I feel obligated not to play favorites when it comes to fruit. However, if I'm forced to be honest, I am most excited each summer by the arrival of apricots. Even a mediocre one sings when cooked down and sweetened slightly. The relatively short cooking time and the gentle sweetness of the honey allow the flavor of the fruit and lavender to sparkle.

MAKES 3 (HALF-PINT/250 ML) JARS

1 dry quart apricots (about 1½ pounds/ 680 g whole fruit), pitted and chopped
¾ cup/255 g honey
2 teaspoons food-grade lavender buds

Stir the apricots and honey together in a medium bowl to combine. Tie up the lavender buds in a length of cheesecloth so that none can escape and tuck it into the apricots and honey. Cover and let sit at room temperature for an hour, so that the lavender flavor can begin to infuse into the fruit.

When the time is up, taste the uncooked mixture. If you like the current level of lavender infusion, remove the packet and discard. If you want a bit more lavender flavor, leave the packet in for the first 10 to 15 minutes of cooking.

Prepare a boiling water bath and 3 half-pint/250 ml jars according to the process on page 11. Place 3 lids in a small saucepan of water and bring to a gentle simmer.

Pour the fruit, honey, and lavender packet into a wide, nonreactive pot. Place over high heat and boil, stirring regularly, for 15 to 20 minutes. Check the consistency regularly by pulling your spatula through the butter and clearing a trail. If it rushes in immediately to fill the space, continue to cook. If the space stays open for a few moments, it is done. Once it passes this thickness test, remove the pot from the heat, and fish out the lavender packet.

Ladle the butter into the prepared jars. Wipe the rims, apply the lids and rings, and process in a boiling water bath for 10 minutes (see pages 11–12).

Note: Preserves sweetened with honey only last 2 to 3 weeks in the fridge once opened. Consider canning this one in quarter-pint/125 ml jars so that the open portion is small.

Apricot Rosemary Jam

My initial motivation to combine apricots with rosemary came from a post on a lovely blog called *Putting By*. I made a batch the same week the recipe was posted and fell hard for the pairing. I've found it makes a wonderful glaze for roast meat or poultry, and if you can it up in small quarter-pint/125 ml jars, it is the exact amount needed for a weeknight roast chicken.

MAKES 3 (HALF-PINT/250 ML) JARS

1 dry quart apricots (1$\frac{1}{2}$ pounds/680 g),
  pitted and mashed
2 cups/400 g granulated sugar
3 tablespoons finely chopped fresh rosemary
Juice of 1 lemon

Prepare a boiling water bath and 3 half-pint/250 ml jars according to the process on page 11. Place 3 lids in a small saucepan of water and bring to a gentle simmer.

Combine the apricots, sugar, and chopped rosemary in a large, nonreactive skillet over medium-high heat. Stirring regularly, bring the fruit to a boil and cook until it bubbles and looks quite thick, 12 to 15 minutes. It's done when you pull a spatula through the jam and it doesn't immediately rush to fill the space you've cleared. When the jam seems thick and spreadable, stir in the lemon juice. Remove the jam from the heat and funnel into the prepared jars, leaving $\frac{1}{2}$ inch/12 mm of headspace. Wipe the rims, apply the lids and rings, and process in a boiling water bath for 10 minutes (see pages 11–12).

Note: Sometimes I mix things up and swap in red chile flakes for the rosemary. Apricots play nicely with a little bit of heat.

Apricot Almond Conserve

onserves are fruit preserves that include either dried fruits or nuts. This honey-sweetened version employs them both, for added flavor and texture. The combination of fresh and dried apricot is particularly nice, as they complement each other and yet still manage to bring distinct virtues to the party. Serve this one at brunch, with a runny cheese and nutty, toasted rolls.

MAKES 2 (HALF-PINT/250 ML) JARS

1 dry quart apricots (about 1 ¹/₂ pounds/680 g)
³/₄ cup/255 g honey
¹/₂ cup/65 g chopped dried apricots
1 cinnamon stick
Zest and juice of ¹/₂ lemon
¹/₃ cup/40 g blanched and slivered almonds, toasted

Prepare a boiling water bath and 2 half-pint/250 ml jars according to the process on page 11. Place 2 lids in a small saucepan of water and bring to a gentle simmer.

Pull the apricots in half, remove the pits, and chop roughly. Combine them with the honey, dried apricots, and cinnamon stick in a medium bowl. Stir to combine and let the fruit macerate for 15 minutes.

To cook, scrape the fruit into a large, nonreactive skillet and place over medium-high heat. Stirring regularly, bring the fruit to a boil and cook until it bubbles and looks quite thick, 10 to 12 minutes. It's done when you pull a spatula through the conserve and it doesn't immediately rush in to fill the space you've cleared.

Remove the saucepan from the heat and stir in the lemon zest, lemon juice, and toasted almonds. Funnel the conserve into the prepared jars, leaving ¹/₂ inch/12 mm of headspace. Wipe the rims, apply the lids and rings, and process in a boiling water bath for 10 minutes (see pages 11–12).

Sweet Cherry Compote

Most of the recipes in this book are designed to use up produce that might otherwise go to waste. This preparation is just a little bit different in that I never, ever have cherries that go wanting for use or attention. If given the opportunity, I can easily eat a pound or two in a single sitting. I have to be intentional about setting aside a quart to make this conserve. Come December, I'm always grateful that I did.

MAKES 2 (HALF-PINT/250 ML) JARS

1 dry quart sweet cherries (about $1\frac{1}{2}$ pounds/680 g)
1 cup/200 g granulated sugar
3 strips lemon zest, minced
$\frac{1}{2}$ teaspoon almond extract

Prepare a boiling water bath and 2 half-pint/250 ml jars according to the process on page 11. Place 2 lids in a small saucepan of water and bring to a gentle simmer.

Pit the cherries, place the fruit in a medium bowl, and add the sugar and lemon zest. Stir to combine and let sit until the sugar has mostly dissolved, about 15 minutes. Scrape the fruit into a medium saucepan.

Set the pan over medium-high heat and simmer, stirring regularly, until the cherries soften a little and a goodly amount of syrup has developed, 4 to 6 minutes. In the last minute of cooking, stir in the almond extract.

Remove the pan from the heat and funnel the compote into the prepared jars, leaving $\frac{1}{2}$ inch/12 mm of headspace. Wipe the rims, apply the lids and rings, and process in a boiling water bath for 10 minutes (see pages 11–12).

Sour Cherries with Bourbon

I was on the road a lot, teaching canning classes, during the summer of 2012 and missed most of cherry season in the Philadelphia area. By the time I got home and was ready to can, I could only scare up a single quart of sour cherries. In pondering the highest use for my solitary container, I settled on this preserve. It lets the cherries play the starring role, with just a little bourbon for enhancement. Add them to cocktails in place of a sickly sweet maraschino or spoon them over vanilla gelato.

MAKES 2 (HALF-PINT/250 ML) JARS

1 dry quart sour cherries (about $1\frac{1}{2}$ pounds/680 g)

1 cup/200 g granulated sugar

2 tablespoons bottled lemon juice

2 tablespoons bourbon

Prepare a boiling water bath and 2 half-pint/250 ml jars according to the process on page 11. Place 2 lids in a small saucepan of water and bring to a gentle simmer.

Remove the pits from the cherries while doing your best to keep them mostly whole. Place in a medium bowl and add the sugar. Stir to combine and let sit until the sugar has mostly dissolved, about 15 minutes. Scrape the fruit into a medium saucepan and add the lemon juice and bourbon. Set the pan over medium-high heat and cook, stirring regularly, until the cherries soften a little and a goodly amount of syrup has developed, 4 to 6 minutes.

Remove the pan from the heat and funnel the cherries and syrup into the prepared jars, leaving $\frac{1}{2}$ inch/12 mm of headspace. Wipe the rims, apply the lids and rings, and process in a boiling water bath for 10 minutes (see pages 11–12).

Salted Brown Sugar Peach Jam

aking sweet things and adding a hint of salt has been all the rage in recent years. While I've long been someone inclined to buck trends, I am firmly on board with this one for just one reason: There's simply no denying it tastes really, really good. I've tried salting a number of jams, and this is the best of the bunch. There's something about the slight caramel-y flavor of the brown sugar that, when coupled with a hint of salt, makes this jam absolutely dreamy.

MAKES 3 (HALF-PINT/250 ML) JARS

1 dry quart peaches (about 2 pounds/910 g)
1 cup/225 g packed light brown sugar
$^3/_4$ teaspoon finely milled sea salt
$^1/_2$ teaspoon freshly grated nutmeg
Juice of $^1/_2$ lemon

Prepare a boiling water bath and 3 half-pint/250 ml jars according to the process on page 11. Place 3 lids in a small saucepan of water and bring to a gentle simmer.

Bring a large pot of water to a boil. While it heats, cut the peaches in half and remove the pits. Fill a large bowl two-thirds of the way up with ice water. Blanch the peaches in the boiling water for 1 to 2 minutes, then immediately transfer to the ice water.

Once they are cool enough to touch, slip off the skins. Place the peaches in a shallow bowl or baking dish. Using a potato masher, smash them into a chunky pulp. Stir in the sugar and let the fruit sit for a few minutes, until the sugar is mostly dissolved.

To cook, scrape the fruit into a large skillet, add the salt, nutmeg, and lemon juice, and place over medium-high heat. Stirring regularly, bring the fruit to a boil and cook until it bubbles and looks quite thick, 10 to 12 minutes. It's done when you pull a spatula through the jam and it doesn't immediately rush in to fill the space you've cleared.

Remove the jam from the heat and funnel into the prepared jars, leaving $^1/_2$ inch/12 mm of headspace. Wipe the rims, apply the lids and rings, and process in a boiling water bath for 10 minutes (see pages 11–12).

Peach Jam with Sriracha

When peaches are in season, I have a hard time holding back and end up buying vast quantities of them. It's always far more than I can eat before they soften precariously and so I'm always devising new ways to put them into jars. A few years back, while cooking up a little batch of peach jam, my eyes fell on the bottle of sriracha sitting on the counter. On a whim, I squirted some into the nearly finished jam, just to see what would happen. The result was a sweet, tart, and slightly spicy jam that is a revelation with turkey burgers and roasted sweet potatoes.

MAKES 3 (HALF-PINT/250 ML) JARS

1 dry quart peaches (about 2 pounds/910 g)
1 cup/200 g granulated sugar
$\frac{1}{4}$ cup/60 ml sriracha
Juice of $\frac{1}{2}$ lemon

Prepare a boiling water bath and 3 half-pint/250 ml jars according to the process on page 11. Place 3 lids in a small saucepan of water and bring to a gentle simmer.

Bring a large pot of water to a boil. While it heats, cut the peaches in half and remove the pits. Fill a large bowl two-thirds of the way up with cold water. Blanch the peaches in the boiling water for 1 to 2 minutes, then immediately transfer to the ice water.

Once they are cool enough to touch, slip off the skins and halve and pit the peaches. Place the peaches in a shallow bowl or baking dish. Using a potato masher, smash them into a pulp. Stir in the sugar and let the fruit sit for a few minutes, until the sugar is mostly dissolved.

To cook, scrape the fruit into a large skillet, add the lemon juice, and place over medium-high heat. Stirring regularly, bring the fruit to a boil and cook until it bubbles and looks quite thick, 10 to 12 minutes. It's done when you pull a spatula through the jam and it doesn't immediately rush in to fill the space you've cleared. In the last couple of minutes of cooking, stir in the sriracha.

Remove the jam from the heat and funnel into the prepared jars, leaving $\frac{1}{2}$ inch/12 mm of headspace. Wipe the rims, apply the lids and rings, and process in a boiling water bath for 10 minutes (see pages 11–12).

Peach Barbecue Sauce

I grew up in a household that was entirely divided on the issue of barbecue sauce. My father was a devotee, whereas my mom can't bear even the faintest whiff of the stuff. I find myself somewhere in between my parents' sauce extremes. This version, made with peaches, is my current favorite. I like to keep the spiciness in check, but chile fiends are welcome to increase the heat to taste.

MAKES 2 (HALF-PINT/250 ML) JARS

1 dry quart yellow peaches (about 2 pounds/910 g)
³/₄ cup/180 ml cider vinegar
¹/₂ cup/115 g packed light brown sugar
¹/₂ cup/80 g minced yellow onion
1 garlic clove, crushed
2 teaspoons smoked paprika
2 teaspoons finely milled sea salt
¹/₂ teaspoon Aleppo pepper
¹/₄ teaspoon cayenne pepper, or to taste

Prepare a small boiling water bath and 2 half-pint/250 ml jars according to the process on page 11. Place 2 lids in a small saucepan of water and bring to a gentle simmer.

Bring a large pot of water to a boil. While it heats, cut the peaches in half and remove the pits. Fill a large bowl with ice water. Blanch the peaches in the boiling water for 1 to 2 minutes, then immediately transfer to the ice water. When cool, remove the peach skins.

Combine all the ingredients in a saucepan with a tight-fitting lid over medium heat and stir to combine. Cover and simmer for about 10 minutes, until the peaches and onion have softened. Using a potato masher, break down the peach pieces. Continue to cook, uncovered, for 40 to 45 minutes, until the mixture has reduced by about half.

Remove the pot from the heat. Using an immersion blender, purée the mixture until smooth (you may have to tip the pan a little to do this). If you don't have an immersion blender, scrape the mixture into a blender or food processor and blend until smooth.

If the sauce is nice and thick, it is done. If it's still a little watery, return it to the heat and cook a bit longer. At this point, taste it and add more salt or pepper, if necessary.

When it's finished, divide the sauce between the prepared jars. Wipe the rims, apply the lids and rings, and process in a boiling water bath for 20 minutes (see pages 11–12).

Pickled Nectarine Slices

T here was a time when pickled fruit was a standard in American homes and pantries. However, over the last 75 years, we've developed something of condiment monoculture. Ketchup was streamlined to mean a sauce made from tomatoes. Relish could no longer contain a world of garden vegetables. And the word "pickle" became synonymous with Kirby cucumbers submerged in tangy brine. I believe it's time return to greater condiment diversity, and there's no better place to start than with these pickled nectarines. They are so good mixed into a salad of tender lettuces or paired with a chunk of Cheddar cheese.

MAKES 4 (HALF-PINT/250 ML) JARS

1 dry quart nectarines (about 2 pounds/910 g)

$1^1/_2$ cups/360 ml distilled white vinegar

$^3/_4$ cup/150 g granulated sugar

2 teaspoons finely milled sea salt

4 star anise

2 cinnamon stick, broken into halves

2 bay leaves, broken into halves

1 teaspoon black peppercorns, divided

Prepare a boiling water bath and 4 half-pint/250 ml jars according to the process on page 11. Place 4 lids in a small saucepan of water and bring to a gentle simmer.

In a medium saucepan, combine the vinegar with $1^1/_2$ cups/360 ml of water, the sugar, and the salt, and bring to a boil.

While the pickling brine comes to temperature, wash the nectarines, then halve and pit. Cut each half into 6 to 8 wedges.

Divide the spices evenly among the prepared jars.

Once the brine is boiling, add the fruit to the pot. Stir to help settle the fruit into the brine. When the brine has returned to a boil, remove the pot from the heat.

Carefully ladle the fruit into the prepared jars, using a wooden chopstick to help the nectarine slices settle into place. Pour the brine over the fruit to cover, leaving $1/_2$ inch/12 mm of headspace. Tap the jars gently to remove any air bubbles and use the chopstick to dislodge any trapped air bubbles.

Wipe the rims, apply the lids and rings, and process in a boiling water bath for 10 minutes (see pages 11–12). The pickled nectarines should be allowed to sit in their brine for at least 48 hours before being eaten.

Note: It's best to use slightly underripe fruit to make these pickles. Truly ripe fruit will dissolve into goo in the jars.

Nectarine Jam with Lemon Verbena and Honey

This recipe was born out of absolute necessity. My husband and I had been on a midsummer road trip through farm country and had paid many a visit to area produce stands. I'd bought far too many nectarines, and when we arrived home, I had a bag of very ripe, almost drippy fruit. Before even starting the first load of laundry, I pitted, chopped (removing bruises along the way), and made a batch of jam very much like this one.

MAKES 2 (HALF-PINT/250 ML) JARS

1 dry quart ripe nectarines, pitted and chopped
  (about 2 pounds/910 g)
$^3/_4$ cup/255 g honey
5 to 6 fresh lemon verbena leaves

Prepare a boiling water bath and 2 half-pint/250 ml jars according to the process on page 11. Place 2 lids in a small saucepan of water and bring to a gentle simmer.

Combine the nectarines, honey, and lemon verbena leaves in a large skillet and place over medium-high heat. Stirring regularly, bring the fruit to a boil and cook until it bubbles and looks quite thick, 10 to 12 minutes. It's done when you pull a spatula through the jam and it doesn't immediately rush in to fill the space you've cleared.

Remove the jam from the heat and funnel into the prepared jars, leaving $^1/_2$ inch/12 mm of headspace. Wipe the rims, apply the lids and rings, and process in a boiling water bath for 10 minutes (see pages 11–12).

Note: This jam can also be made with peaches, plums, and apricots. If you're feeling adventurous or need to use up a few odds and ends, feel free to turn it into a mixed stone fruit jam.

Sandwich Bar

My parents moved us from Southern California to Portland, Oregon, just before my ninth birthday. Once we settled in, nearly everything about life in the Pacific Northwest was better and easier. It quickly became the case that the only thing that anyone missed about California was the extended family we left behind.

And so once a summer, my parents would rent a roomy house in Florence, Oregon, for a week and invite everyone, family and close friends alike. Once the house was full, we'd settle into a comfortable pattern of lazy days and very regular meals. Every morning, people would gather for breakfast, before going off to walk on the beach, wander through the antique stores in town, or construct massive sand sculptures. Lunch was a hodgepodge of leftovers, snacks, and fruit. Then, around three in the afternoon, a few people would gather and start talking about the plan for dinner.

If there'd been a crabbing excursion that day, all that was needed was coleslaw, corn, and melted butter. At least one night, we'd build a bonfire on the beach and roast hot dogs and marshmallows on sticks. The meal I always looked forward to most was the night that my Aunt Lolly would coordinate a make-your-own sandwich bar.

She always brought several loaves of fresh sourdough bread up from San Francisco with her, and then would hit the local deli for the fixings. All the regular sandwich ingredients would be present, including turkey, roast beef, tuna salad, and three kinds of sliced cheese. There'd be plenty of sliced tomato, red onion, sprouts, lettuce leaves, cucumber rounds, and mashed avocado (for those who don't like mayonnaise, it moistens beautifully).

Just when you thought your sandwich was finished, there at the end of the table were the pickles. This wasn't just an ordinary jar of kosher dills. We had sweet-and-sour gherkins, pickled okra (a favorite of my grandma Bunny), sour green tomatoes, still-crunchy quick-pickled red onions, a jar of garden relish, and squeeze bottle filled with herb vinaigrette (for a final dash of pucker). It was a pickle paradise.

The vinaigrette came from my mom's best friend Maria. For most of the 1980s and 1990s, she and her husband owned a small chain of cafés where they sold made-to-order sandwiches, all topped with this vinaigrette. She and her family were often present at these beach gatherings, and they always brought a large batch for sandwich and salad dressing.

Once everyone had a sandwich, we'd file down the gritty wooden steps that led from the deck down to the beach and watch the sun set over the Pacific Ocean. With potato chips crunching and the waves crashing, those were some of the very happiest nights of my childhood.

Herb Vinaigrette

MAKES 1 CUP/240 ML

$^2/_3$ cup/160 ml extra-virgin olive oil
3 tablespoons red wine vinegar
3 tablespoons freshly squeezed lemon juice
2 garlic cloves, minced
2 teaspoons dried basil
2 teaspoons dry mustard
1 teaspoon sea salt
$^1/_4$ teaspoon freshly ground black pepper

In a blender, combine the olive oil, vinegar, lemon juice, garlic, basil, mustard, salt, and pepper. Blend until just incorporated and pour into a mason jar for storage. It will keep in the refrigerator for up to 2 weeks.

Note: Part of what made this dressing so magical for me was the fact that it came to these gatherings in a food-service squeeze bottle. It's the perfect applicator, because it allows you to squirt just the right amount of vinaigrette to the sandwich.

Blueberry Jam
with Crystallized Ginger

credit blueberries for my transformation from basic cook to obsessive home canner. Now I don't let a year go by without making a couple different batches of blueberry jam. I often make it just the way my mom still does, flavored with cinnamon, nutmeg, and lemon zest. In recent years, I've added this very gingery version to my repertoire and now I can't imagine going a season without.

MAKES 2 (HALF-PINT/250 ML) JARS

1 dry quart fresh blueberries, rinsed, picked over, and mashed (about 1$\frac{1}{2}$ pounds/680 g)

1 cup/200 g granulated sugar

1 tablespoon grated fresh ginger (about 3 inches)

Juice of $\frac{1}{2}$ lemon

$\frac{1}{4}$ cup/40 g chopped crystallized ginger

Prepare a boiling water bath and 2 half-pint/250 ml jars according to the process on page 11. Place 2 lids in a small saucepan of water and bring to a gentle simmer.

Combine the blueberries, sugar, ginger, and lemon juice in a large skillet. Stir to help the sugar dissolve. Once the mixture has begun to look syrupy, place the skillet over medium-high heat.

Stirring regularly, bring the fruit to a boil and cook until it bubbles and looks quite thick, 10 to 12 minutes. It's done when you pull a spatula through the jam and it doesn't immediately rush in to fill the space you've cleared.

When the jam is finished cooking, remove the pot from the heat and stir in the candied ginger. Pour into the prepared jars. Wipe the rims, apply the lids and rings, and process in a boiling water bath for 10 minutes (see pages 11–12).

Blueberry Maple Jam

ne of my favorite food blogs is one called *Well Preserved*. Written by Canadians Dana Harrison and Joel MacCharles, it features a wealth of useful, clear, and inspiring preserving information. This recipe is a very slightly adapted version of a jam they refer to as "blueberry crack," sweet and with a primal maple essence. I like to dollop it on pancakes in place of my standard drizzle of syrup.

MAKES 2 (HALF-PINT/250 ML) JARS

1 dry quart fresh blueberries, rinsed, picked over, and mashed, (about 1$\frac{1}{2}$ pounds/680 g)
$\frac{3}{4}$ cup/175 g packed light brown sugar
$\frac{1}{2}$ cup/120 ml pure maple syrup
2 tablespoons bottled lemon juice

Prepare a boiling water bath and 2 half-pint/250 ml jars according to the process on page 11. Place 2 lids in a small saucepan of water and bring to a gentle simmer.

Combine the blueberries, sugar, maple syrup, and lemon juice in a large skillet. Stir to help the sugar dissolve and to integrate the maple syrup. Once the mixture has begun to look syrupy, place the skillet over medium-high heat and bring to a boil.

Stirring regularly, bring the fruit to a boil and cook until it bubbles and looks quite thick, 10 to 12 minutes. It's done when you pull a spatula through the jam and it doesn't immediately rush in to fill the space you've cleared.

When the jam is finished cooking, remove the pot from the heat and pour into the prepared jars. Wipe the rims, apply the lids and rings, and process in a boiling water bath for 10 minutes (see pages 11–12).

Note: Because maple syrup has a lower acidity than sugar, it's important to use bottled lemon juice in this recipe to ensure that the acid levels remain safe for boiling water bath canning.

Pickled Wax Beans

This pickle is a take on the traditional dilly beans, which are most often made with green beans. A few years back, I had a share in a CSA that ended up including multitudinous wax beans. After eating all I could manage steamed and buttered, I turned to pickling and was delighted to discover that they were just as good in brine as their green brethren. Because wax beans are sturdy little suckers, they retain their crispness through the boiling water bath process.

MAKES 4 (HALF-PINT/250 ML) JARS

1 dry quart wax beans (about $1\frac{1}{2}$ pounds/680 g)
$1\frac{1}{2}$ cups/360 ml cider vinegar
2 tablespoons finely milled sea salt
4 medium-size garlic cloves, divided
4 teaspoons dill seeds, divided
2 teaspoons black peppercorns, divided

Prepare a boiling water bath and 4 half-pint/250 ml jars according to the process on page 11. Place 4 lids in a small saucepan of water and bring to a gentle simmer.

Wash and trim the beans so that they fit in the jars. If you have particularly long beans, cut them in half. Combine the vinegar, $1\frac{1}{2}$ cups/360 ml of water, and the salt in a medium saucepan and bring to a boil. While the pickling liquid heats, pack your beans into the jars, leaving $\frac{1}{2}$ inch/12 mm of headspace. To each jar, add 1 garlic clove, 1 teaspoon of dill seeds, and $\frac{1}{2}$ teaspoon of peppercorns.

Slowly pour the hot brine over the beans, leaving $\frac{1}{2}$ inch/12 mm of headspace. After all the jars are full, use a wooden chopstick to dislodge any trapped air bubbles. Add more liquid to return the headspace to $\frac{1}{2}$ inch/12 mm, if necessary. Wipe the rims, apply the lids and rings, and process in a boiling water bath for 10 minutes (see pages 11–12). Let the pickles sit for at least a week before eating.

Note: You can really use any combination of beans you have, for this pickle. I'm particularly fond of choosing several different colors of beans and mixing them in a single jar. Even flat Romano beans do well here.

Garlic Dill Pickle Spears

Here in the United States, cucumbers are inextricably linked to pickles. While there's no rule that cucumbers are the only vegetable that can be pickled, there's a reason they're so popular. They're damn good. I feel my fridge is somehow incomplete without a jar of cucumber dills for munching, crunching, and dicing for tuna salad. This is my favorite basic fridge pickle. Maybe it will become yours as well.

MAKES 2 (1-PINT/500 ML) JARS

1 dry quart Kirby cucumbers (about 1$\frac{1}{2}$ pounds/680 g)
$\frac{3}{4}$ cup/360 ml cider vinegar
2 teaspoons finely milled sea salt
2 teaspoons dill seeds
4 garlic cloves, peeled
2 green onions (whites only), chopped

Wash and dry the cucumbers. Chop off the ends and slice into spears. Combine the vinegar, 3/4 cup/180 ml of water, and the salt in a saucepan and bring to a boil.

Equally divide the dill seeds, garlic cloves, and onion between 2 (1-pint/500 ml) jars. Pack the cucumber spears into the jars as tightly as you can without crushing them.

Pour the brine into the jars, leaving $\frac{1}{4}$ inch/6 mm of headspace. Tap the jars gently and wiggle the cucumbers with a wooden chopstick to dislodge any trapped air bubbles. Add more liquid to return the headspace to $\frac{1}{4}$ inch/6 mm, if necessary. Wipe the rims, apply the lids and rings, and let the jars cool on the countertop. Once they're cool, put them in the refrigerator. Let cure for at least a day before eating. The pickles will keep in the fridge for up to a month.

Black Plum Chutney

O ne of the things that makes chutney so useful in a preserver's toolbox is the fact that it is fairly fuss-free. Sure, there's some chopping involved before the ingredients are ready for the pot, but once they're on the stove, all you have to do is cook over moderate heat and stir occasionally. The result is a slightly sweet, sharp, savory preserve that is happy to enhance toasted cheese sandwiches, roasted meat, and even just a bowl of steamed brown rice.

MAKES 3 (HALF-PINT/250 ML) JARS

1 dry quart black plums, pitted and diced
   (about 2 pounds/910 g)
1 cup/170 g golden raisins
3/4 cup/120 g chopped yellow onion
Zest and juice of 1 lemon
1 cup/240 ml cider vinegar
1 cup/225 g light brown sugar
1 (1-inch piece) fresh ginger, peeled and grated
2 teaspoons mustard seeds
1 teaspoon ground cloves
1 cinnamon stick
1/2 teaspoon red chile flakes

Combine the plums, raisins, onion, lemon zest and juice, vinegar, sugar, ginger, mustard seeds, cloves, cinnamon stick, and chile flakes in a wide saucepan, stir to combine, and bring to a vigorous boil. Lower the heat to medium and cook, stirring often, until the mixture has reduced and developed a thick, spreadable consistency, 45 to 55 minutes.

When the chutney is halfway through cooking, prepare a boiling water bath and 3 half-pint/250 ml jars according to the process on page 11. Place 3 lids in a small saucepan of water and bring to a gentle simmer.

Once the chutney is quite thick and the flavors are well integrated, remove the pan from the heat. Fish out the cinnamon stick and discard. Ladle the chutney into the prepared jars, leaving 1/2 inch/12 mm of headspace. Wipe the rims, apply the lids and rings, and process in a boiling water bath for 15 minutes (see pages 11–12).

Italian Plum Jam with Star Anise

first made this jam years back, late in the summer season. The fruit was rapidly softening and very sweet and couldn't wait another day to be used. I chopped the fruit into bits, added a bit less than half as much sugar as usual and popped in a few pieces of star anise on a whim. The finished jam was ridiculously good. The next day, I dashed out in the hopes of finding more Italian plums, but they had been the very last ones. I appreciated that small batch all the more for its scarcity and managed to make it last until those plums returned again.

MAKES 2 (HALF-PINT/250 ML) JARS

1 pound/460 g Italian plums, pitted and chopped
$^3/_4$ cup/150 g granulated sugar
3 star anise

Combine the plums, sugar, and star anise in a small bowl. Let sit for at least an hour, to give the anise flavor a chance to infuse into the fruit.

Prepare a boiling water bath and 2 half-pint/250 ml jars according to the process on page 11. Place 2 lids in a small saucepan of water and bring to a gentle simmer.

To cook, scrape the fruit into a large skillet and place over medium-high heat. Stirring regularly, bring the fruit to a boil and cook until it bubbles and looks quite thick, 10 to 12 minutes. It's done when you pull a spatula through the jam and it doesn't immediately rush in to fill the space you've cleared.

Remove the jam from the heat and funnel into the prepared jars, leaving $^1/_2$ inch/12 mm of headspace. Wipe the rims, apply the lids and rings, and process in a boiling water bath for 10 minutes (see pages 11–12).

Yellow Plum Jam
with Vanilla

Plum jam tastes like childhood to me. When I was very young, my family lived in a house with three plum trees (two red, one yellow) scattered around the yard and every other year, we spent three weeks wading through a sea of plums. We'd eat them until we couldn't bear to look at another and then my mom would make enough jam to last until the trees ripened again.

MAKES 2 (HALF-PINT/250 ML) JARS

1 dry quart yellow plums (about 2 pounds/910 g)
1$\frac{1}{2}$ cups/300 g granulated sugar
1 vanilla bean, split and scraped
Juice of $\frac{1}{2}$ lemon

Prepare a boiling water bath and 2 half-pint/250 ml jars according to the process on page 11. Place 2 lids in a small saucepan of water and bring to a gentle simmer.

Wash, pit, and chop the plums. Place them in a medium bowl with the sugar and vanilla seeds and bean. Let the fruit rest for 20 to 30 minutes.

To cook, scrape the fruit into a large skillet, add the lemon juice, and place over medium-high heat. Stirring regularly, bring the fruit to a boil and cook until it bubbles and looks quite thick, 10 to 12 minutes. It's done when you pull a spatula through the jam and it doesn't immediately rush in to fill the space you've cleared.

Remove the jam from the heat and fish out the vanilla bean. Funnel into the prepared jars, leaving $\frac{1}{2}$ inch/12 mm of headspace. Wipe the rims, apply the lids and rings, and process in a boiling water bath for 10 minutes (see pages 11–12).

Raspberry Habanero Jam

I've always been of the opinion that when it comes to preserving raspberries, the simplest approach is the best. And so, I typically make my jam with just enough sugar to ensure a set and a squirt of lemon juice for balance. But once while wandering a farmers' market, I happened on a vendor selling homemade jams. She had a spicy raspberry jelly that made my eyes water. Once the burn faded, I realized that there was something about the way the raspberry and the peppery heat went together that made me want to try it in my own kitchen. Combined with a little cider vinegar, it makes an excellent glaze for chicken wings.

MAKES 2 (HALF-PINT/250 ML) JARS

1 dry quart raspberries (about 1$\frac{1}{2}$ pounds/680 g)
1$\frac{1}{2}$ cups/300 g granulated sugar
1 habañero pepper, sliced along the sides
Juice of $\frac{1}{2}$ lemon

Prepare a boiling water bath and 2 half-pint/250 ml jars according to the process on page 11. Place 2 lids in a small saucepan of water and bring to a gentle simmer.

In a medium bowl, combine the raspberries and sugar. Using a wooden spoon, stir the sugar into the fruit, mashing up the fruit a bit as you go. Once the raspberries begin to release some juice and the sugar is starting to dissolve, scrape the berry mixture into a large skillet. Add the hot pepper.

Bring the jam to a boil over high heat, stirring regularly, until the berries break down and the syrup thickens. You should smell both the sweetness of the sugar and the heat of the pepper. It's done when you pull a spatula through the jam and it doesn't immediately rush in to fill the space you've cleared.

Remove the jam from the heat and fish out the spent habañero. Funnel into the prepared jars, leaving $\frac{1}{2}$ inch/12 mm of headspace. Wipe the rims, apply the lids and rings, and process in a boiling water bath for 10 minutes (see pages 11–12).

Black Raspberry Preserves

lthough my home state of Oregon is responsible for the bulk of the black raspberry production in the United States, I didn't discover them until I moved to Pennsylvania. Also known as black caps, they are much beloved around these parts and are believed by many to make superior pies and preserves. Because they're quite rare, they can also be shockingly expensive. To help cushion the financial blow, I tend to preserve them in truly tiny batches and consider myself lucky to have them at all.

MAKES 2 (QUARTER-PINT/125 ML) JARS

1 pint black raspberries (about 12 ounces/340 g)
$^2/_3$ cup/130 g granulated sugar
1 teaspoon freshly squeezed lemon juice

Prepare a boiling water bath and 2 quarter-pint/125 ml jars according to the process on page 11. Place 2 lids in a small saucepan of water and bring to a gentle simmer.

Tumble the black raspberries into a small bowl and mash them with a fork. Add the sugar and lemon juice and stir to combine. Let the fruit sit for a few minutes, until the sugar begins to dissolve.

To cook, scrape the fruit into a large skillet and place over medium-high heat. Stirring regularly, bring the fruit to a boil and cook until it bubbles and looks quite thick, 5 to 8 minutes. It's done when you pull a spatula through the jam and it doesn't immediately rush in to fill the space you've cleared.

Remove the jam from the heat and funnel into the prepared jars, leaving $^1/_2$ inch/12 mm of headspace. Wipe the rims, apply the lids and rings, and process in a boiling water bath for 10 minutes (see pages 11–12).

Note: This very basic jam recipe can be used for nearly any costly, precious berry. Try it with red raspberries, blackberries, salmonberries, or olallieberries, minding the ratios.

Seedy Spiced Blackberry Jam

Every summer, my mom makes dozens of jars of jam to sell at a select handful of fall craft shows. One of her most popular flavors is her spiced blackberry. She and my dad spend hours foraging wild blackberries for the jam. Once home, she pushes the berries through a fine-mesh sieve to remove the seeds and adds plenty of warm spices during cooking. Although it's been years since we canned together, I still make mine in much the same way. Truly, the only difference is that I've come to appreciate the texture of the seeds and so leave them in. It's an added bonus that skipping the seed removal means even less work to go from fruit to jam.

MAKES 2 (HALF-PINT/250 ML) JARS

1 dry quart blackberries, (about 1 $^{1}\!/_{2}$ pounds/680 g)
1 cup/200 g granulated sugar
1 teaspoon ground cinnamon
$^{1}\!/_{2}$ teaspoon freshly grated nutmeg
Zest and juice of $^{1}\!/_{2}$ lemon

Prepare a boiling water bath and 2 half-pint/250 ml jars according to the process on page 11. Place 2 lids in a small saucepan of water and bring to a gentle simmer.

In a medium bowl, combine the blackberries and sugar. Using a wooden spoon, stir the sugar into the fruit, mashing up the fruit a bit as you go. Once the blackberries begin to release some juice and the sugar is starting to dissolve, scrape the berry mixture into a large skillet. Add the cinnamon, nutmeg, and lemon juice and zest.

Bring the jam to a boil over high heat, stirring regularly, until the berries break down and the syrup thickens. It's done when you pull a spatula through the jam and it doesn't immediately rush in to fill the space you've cleared.

Remove the jam from the heat. Funnel into the prepared jars, leaving $^{1}\!/_{2}$ inch/12 mm of headspace. Wipe the rims, apply the lids and rings, and process in a boiling water bath for 10 minutes (see pages 11–12).

Preserved Fig Quarters with Whiskey

Philadelphia is full of feral fig trees, some planted by long-gone Italian immigrants. If you know where to look and your timing is good, it is possible to fill a gallon bucket. I tend to restrain myself and pick just a pound or two from these community trees, to ensure that others can also have a share. Then I bring them home and make this preserve.

MAKES 2 (HALF-PINT/250 ML) JARS

1 pound/460 g figs
1 cup/200 g granulated sugar
2 tablespoons bottled lemon juice
2 tablespoons whiskey

Prepare a boiling water bath and 2 half-pint/250 ml jars according to the process on page 11. Place 2 lids in a small saucepan of water and bring to a gentle simmer.

Trim away any woody stems from the figs and cut them into quarters. Place in a medium bowl and add the sugar. Stir to combine and let sit until the sugar has mostly dissolved. Scrape the fruit into a medium saucepan and add the lemon juice and whiskey. Set the pan over medium-high heat and cook, stirring regularly, until the figs soften and a goodly amount of syrup has developed, 4 to 6 minutes.

When the figs are tender but not cooked to mush, they are finished. Remove the pan from the heat and funnel the figs and syrup into the prepared jars, leaving ½ inch/12 mm of headspace. Wipe the rims, apply the lids and rings, and process in a boiling water bath for 10 minutes (see pages 11–12).

Marinated Red Peppers

When I was seventeen, my next-door neighbor Alma taught me how to roast red peppers. She used the open flame on her old enamel gas stove to blister the skin of the peppers, then slid the skins off under running water. I cook on a gas stove, so I can't make my peppers exactly like Alma's, but I think of her when I eat these.

MAKES 2 (HALF-PINT/250 ML) JARS

$1\frac{1}{2}$ pounds/680 g red bell peppers
$\frac{1}{4}$ cup/60 ml bottled lemon juice
$\frac{3}{4}$ cup/180 ml white wine vinegar
$\frac{1}{4}$ cup/60 ml olive oil
$1\frac{1}{2}$ teaspoons granulated sugar
$\frac{1}{2}$ teaspoon Aleppo pepper
$\frac{1}{2}$ teaspoon salt
$\frac{1}{4}$ teaspoon freshly ground black pepper

Prepare a boiling water bath and 2 half-pint/250 ml jars according to the process on page 11. Place 2 lids in a small saucepan of water and bring to a gentle simmer.

Heat your oven's broiler to high. Cover a rimmed baking sheet with aluminum foil, place the peppers on the pan, and slide the pan under the broiler. Cook the peppers for 1 to 2 minutes per side under the broiler, until they are uniformly charred and they have collapsed inside their skins. Remove the pan from the broiler and cover the peppers with another length of aluminum foil. Let the peppers rest until cool enough to handle.

While the peppers cool, make the pickling liquid. Combine the lemon juice, vinegar, olive oil, sugar, Aleppo pepper, salt, and black pepper in a medium saucepan. Bring to a boil and then lower the heat to low to keep the brine warm until the peppers are prepped. Once the peppers are cool, peel away the skin and remove the seeds and cores.

Tightly pack the peeled peppers into the prepared jars and cover with the pickling liquid, leaving a generous $\frac{1}{2}$ inch/12 mm of headspace. Using a wooden chopstick, gently prod the peppers to dislodge any trapped air bubbles. Add more liquid to return the headspace to $\frac{1}{2}$ inch/12 mm, if necessary. When the jars are nicely packed, wipe the rims, apply the lids and rings, and process in a boiling water bath for 15 minutes (see pages 11–12).

Bread-and-Butter Zucchini Pickles

n late summer, when the zucchini plants begin to explode, do yourself a favor and make up a batch of this pickle. I find that zucchini does far better than cucumbers in this particular application, absorbing plenty of flavor and staying nicely crisp. We eat it with roast chicken all winter long.

MAKES 4 (HALF-PINT/250 ML) JARS

1 cup/240 ml cider vinegar

½ cup/170 g honey

1 tablespoon mustard seeds

1 teaspoon celery seeds

½ teaspoon red chile flakes

½ teaspoon ground cumin

1 tablespoon finely milled sea salt

1 pound/460 g young zucchini, thickly sliced

1 cup/150 g sliced and seeded red bell pepper

1 cup/160 g sliced onion

Prepare a boiling water bath and 4 half-pint/250 ml jars according to the process on page 11. Place 4 lids in a small saucepan of water and bring to a gentle simmer.

In a medium saucepan, combine the vinegar and honey. Heat until the honey is dissolved. Add the mustard seeds, celery seeds, chile flakes, cumin, and salt and bring to a boil. Once the liquid is rolling, add the zucchini, red pepper, and onion. Stir to combine and cook for 5 minutes, until everything is fully heated through.

Using tongs, divide the vegetables among the prepared jars. Top with the brine, leaving ½ inch/12 mm of headspace. After all the jars are full, use a wooden chopstick to dislodge any trapped air bubbles. Add more liquid to return the headspace to ½ inch/12 mm, if necessary. Wipe the jar rims, apply the lids and rings, and process in a boiling water bath for 10 minutes (see pages 11–12). Let these pickles cure for at least a week prior to eating them.

Zucchini Butter
with Fresh Thyme

I learned to cook zucchini like this from my friend Lucy. At the time, she worked as a flower gardener at a historical home in Virginia. On stormy days, the outdoor staff would gather in their little kitchen and cook up produce from the garden. During one of those cooking sessions, an Italian vegetable gardener taught her to slow cook zucchini with herbs until it melted into a spreadable, succulent paste. I've never been more grateful for a secondhand cooking lesson, as this humble little butter is intensely delicious. I like to spread it on toast or toss it with warm pasta.

MAKES 2 (HALF-PINT/250 ML) JARS

3 tablespoons olive oil

1 tablespoon unsalted butter

5 garlic cloves, gently smashed

2 large zucchini, cut into $\frac{1}{2}$-inch/5 cm cubes
(about 2 pounds/910 g)

5 to 6 springs thyme

$\frac{1}{2}$ teaspoon finely milled sea salt

$\frac{1}{4}$ teaspoon freshly ground black pepper

Place a large skillet over medium heat. Place the olive oil and butter in the pan and allow them to melt together. Roughly chop the garlic and add it to the pan. Add the zucchini. Cook for 15 to 20 minutes, until the zucchini has begun to soften. Strip the thyme leaves off their stems and add them to the pan.

Lower the heat to medium-low and continue to cook, stirring often. The goal is to cook the liquid out of the zucchini and melt it into a flavorful, spreadable paste. If at any point, the zucchini starts to brown and stick, add a splash of liquid (water is fine, though if you have an open bottle, a little white wine is also delicious) and lower the heat a bit more. The total cooking time should be right around an hour.

Divide the cooked spread between 2 half-pint/250 ml jars. It will keep for up to 2 weeks in the fridge or a year in the freezer.

Salt-Preserved Herbs

his technique for salt-preserved herbs requires just herbs, salt, and a jar. It doesn't initially seem like it should work, because all you've done is toss chopped herbs with salt and pack it all in a jar. But it becomes a magic, savory, flavor-giving thing that can last in your fridge indefinitely. I use this mix in soups, stews, braises, pots of beans, and anywhere that could stand extra oomph.

MAKES 1 (1-PINT/500 ML) JAR

8 ounces/230 g mixed fresh herbs
   (parsley, cilantro, basil, chervil, sorrel,
   and leafy celery tops are all good choices)
6 ounces/180 g coarse sea salt

Wash and dry the herbs well. Pluck the leaves from the stems and roughly chop them by hand (a food processor often turns them to paste). Scrape the herbs into a bowl and add the salt. Using clean hands, toss the herbs and salt together until well combined.

Funnel the herb mixture into a 1-quart/1-liter jar, apply a lid, and place it in the fridge. Every day for a week, give it a good shake. At the end of the week, it should have reduced in volume by about half. Transfer the herb salt to a 1-pint/500 ml jar and fit with an airtight lid. It will keep in the refrigerator indefinitely.

Note: When dipping into your jar of herb salt, make sure to only use meticulously clean spoons. This practice extends the life span of your herb salt because there is less risk of introducing any bacteria into the jar.

Thai Basil Pesto

Through the spring, summer, and fall, I like to stock my freezer with little jars of homemade pesto. For years I stuck to the familiar formula of basil, nuts, cheese, and oil. But then a friend turned me on to the idea of trying other flavor families and this Asian-inspired version was born. Toss it with soba noodles and top with chicken or tofu and dinner is served.

MAKES 1 (HALF-PINT/250 ML) JAR

2 cups/80 g fresh Thai basil leaves
$\frac{1}{4}$ cup/40 g peanuts, toasted
1 tablespoon honey
2 tablespoons toasted sesame oil
1 tablespoon yellow miso paste
1 tablespoon unseasoned rice vinegar
1 teaspoon crushed red chile flakes
2 garlic cloves

Combine the basil leaves, peanuts, sesame oil, miso paste, rice vinegar, chile flakes, and garlic in the bowl of a food processor. Run the motor until a paste forms. Remove the lid and scrape down the sides of the processor, if necessary.

Spoon the pesto into a half-pint/250 ml jar and refrigerate or freeze. It will keep for up to a week in the fridge and up to a year in the freezer.

Orange Tomato and Smoked Paprika Jam

started making tomato jam several years back, after a friend gave me a jar of her homemade version. I emptied that little jar in record time and quickly made my own batch. Now it's one of my annual must-haves, and in addition to the classic version, I've come up with a few variations. This is a recent favorite take that pairs sweet orange tomatoes with just a little bit of bold, smoked paprika. If you like a little campfire in your jam, this one is most decidedly for you.

MAKES 3 (HALF-PINT/250 ML) JARS

1 dry quart (about 2 pounds/910 g)
 orange grape tomatoes, chopped
1¼ cups/250 g granulated sugar
¼ cup/60 ml bottled lemon juice
2 tablespoons cider vinegar
1½ teaspoons finely milled sea salt
1½ teaspoons red chile flakes
1 teaspoon grated fresh ginger
1 teaspoon smoked paprika
¼ teaspoon cayenne pepper

Combine the tomatoes, sugar, lemon juice, vinegar, salt, chile flakes, ginger, paprika, and cayenne in a large, nonreactive pot. Bring to a boil and then lower the temperature to a simmer. Stirring regularly, gently boil the jam until it reduces to a sticky, jammy mess. Boiled at a fairly rapid pace, it should take about 45 minutes of cooking.

When the jam is nearly done, prepare a boiling water bath and 3 half-pint/250 ml jars according to the process on page 11. Place 3 lids in a small saucepan of water and bring to a gentle simmer.

When the jam has cooked down sufficiently, remove from the heat and fill the jars, leaving ½ inch/12 mm of headspace. Wipe the rims, apply the lids and rings, and process in a boiling water bath for 15 minutes (see pages 11–12).

Blender Salsa

Fresh, homemade salsa is one of my summertime refrigerator staples. Sadly, its season is painfully short and so I also make salsa for canning when tomatoes are cheap and good. I like this blender version, because the prep is easy, the cooking time is short, and it tastes awfully good on scrambled eggs and toasted corn tortillas with cheese.

MAKES 4 (HALF-PINT/250 ML) JARS

1 dry quart (about 2 pounds/910 g)
  Roma tomatoes, cored and peeled
$1/2$ cup/80 g minced yellow onion
2 garlic cloves, roughly chopped
1 jalapeño pepper, stem and seeds removed, roughly chopped
2 tablespoons bottled lime juice
Zest of 1 lime
2 teaspoons kosher salt
$1/2$ teaspoon citric acid

Prepare a boiling water bath and 4 half-pint/250 ml jars according to the process on page 11. Place 4 lids in a small saucepan of water and bring to a gentle simmer.

Place all the ingredients in a blender (or food processor, if that's what you've got) and blend in short bursts until the ingredients are well incorporated. Don't process to the point of having a smooth purée; you want a salsa that still has a little texture.

Pour the salsa into a medium saucepan and bring to a boil over high heat. Lower the heat to medium-low and simmer for 5 minutes.

Funnel the salsa into the prepared jars. Wipe the rims, apply the lids and rings, and process in a boiling water bath for 15 minutes (see pages 11–12).

Slow-Roasted Grape Tomato Spread

During the summer months, I buy pints of small tomatoes the way other women buy shoes. I am charmed by their size, their many hues, and their sweet, acidic taste. It is only after I arrive home that I remember that I'm the only tomato eater in my household and that there are already two slightly wrinkly pints of tomatoes in the kitchen. Whenever this happens, I make this spread. It extends the life of those tomatoes and is a dream painted inside omelets or tossed with hot pasta and blobs of creamy goat cheese. And in January, when I discover a jar half hidden in the freezer, I sing praises to my summertime self.

MAKES 1 (HALF-PINT/250 ML) JAR

1 pint grape tomatoes, (about 12 ounces/350 g)
5 large garlic cloves
3 sprigs thyme
2 tablespoons olive oil, plus more to cover
1 teaspoon finely milled sea salt
Freshly ground black pepper

Preheat the oven to 300°F/150°C. Wash the tomatoes and spread out on a small rimmed cookie sheet. Scatter the unpeeled garlic cloves and thyme sprigs around tomatoes. Drizzle with the 2 tablespoons of olive oil and adjust the seasoning to taste.

Roast for 20 to 25 minutes, until the tomatoes are tender and shriveled. Remove from the oven and let cool. Scrape the roasted tomatoes into the bowl of a food processor and pulse until you have a chunky purée. Spoon the purée into a half-pint/250 ml jar and cover with a thin layer of olive oil. This tomato spread will keep in the refrigerator for 5 days and in the freezer for up to a year.

Corn and Tomato Relish

I call this recipe a relish because I tend to use it in relish-y places, such as on top of hot dogs or spooned over pieces of oven-baked bluefish. However, because it's got something of a kick, thanks to the presence of the jalapeño, it can also do double duty as a slightly sweet salsa. Try it on top of nachos or strewn across a homemade taco salad.

MAKES 3 (HALF-PINT/250 ML) JARS

3 to 4 ears of corn (for about 2 cups/300 g kernels)
1 cup/180 g peeled and diced tomatoes
$^1/_2$ cup/80 g seeded and diced red bell pepper
$^1/_4$ cup/40 g minced onion
2 teaspoons minced jalapeño pepper
1 cup/240 ml cider vinegar
$^1/_3$ cup/65 g granulated sugar
1 teaspoon yellow mustard seeds
1 teaspoon ground cumin
$^1/_2$ teaspoon finely milled sea salt

Prepare a boiling water bath and 3 half-pint/250 ml jars according to the process on page 11. Place 3 lids in a small saucepan of water and bring to a gentle simmer.

Pour 2 inches/5 cm of water into a lidded pot large enough to hold the ears of corn and bring to a boil. Shuck the corn and steam the cobs for 5 minutes. Cut the kernels away from the cobs (you should have about 2 cups/300 g of corn).

Combine the corn, tomatoes, peppers, onion, jalapeños, cider vinegar, sugar, cumin, mustard seeds, and salt in a medium saucepan over medium-high heat and bring to a boil. Cook at a boil, stirring occasionally, for 8 to 10 minutes, until some of the liquid has evaporated and the tomatoes are quite soft.

When the relish is finished cooking, remove it from the heat. Funnel into the prepared jars, leaving $^1/_2$ inch/12 mm of headspace. Wipe the rims, apply the lids and rings, and process in a boiling water bath for 15 minutes (see pages 11–12).

Fall

RECIPES

My fondest fall memories revolve around the Bybee-
Howell House on Sauvie Island, just outside of Portland, Oregon. The island is
mostly an agricultural community and the Bybee-Howell House was built by the
island's earliest settlers. During the years that I was growing up in that area, it was
maintained as an attraction for visitors, run by the state historical society. Sadly,
budget cuts have since forced it to close. There was an antique apple orchard on
the property and several looming pear trees that produced fruit weighing two or
three pounds each and that took many months to ripen. We were told this variety
was cultivated to ripen this way so they could be taken on long sea voyages.

Each October, there would be a Wintering-In festival on the grounds, to cel-
ebrate the bounty of the harvest and to prepare for winter. There would be historical reenactors teaching lessons in candle and soap making, vendors selling
handmade pottery, old-fashioned toys, vintage photographs, and plenty of
grilled sausages and smoked meats for sale (all made on-site in the old summer
kitchen). Local bluegrass bands provided appropriately old-timey music.

My favorite part of the event was making fresh cider using a press that had been
at the farm since its earliest days. First thing in the morning, volunteers would go
out and harvest the bulk of the apples from the orchard. The freshly picked apples
would be washed, forced through a grinder, and loaded into the barrel of the press.
The adults would trade off the task of turning the wheel that controlled the press
and soon enough, apple cider would come streaming down the angled wooden
board. Because we were too little to help with the actual pressing, all the kids would
be allowed to hold our cups near spout and catch sips of the sweet, fresh cider.

To me, fall preserving should feel like those Wintering-In festivals; abundant
and celebratory. Since most crops of autumn typically keep better and longer
than the fleeting fruit of summer, you can approach these recipes with a bit
less urgency and more leisure.

Fig Jam with Thyme
Pickled Hot Pepper Rings
Pickled Eggplant with Mint
Pickled Crookneck Slices
Red Tomato Pickle
Green Tomato Salsa
Pizza Sauce
Lacto-Fermented Green Tomato Pickle
Quick Pickled Fennel with Orange
Pickled Kohlrabi Matchsticks
Smooth Tomatillo Simmer Sauce
Pear Cranberry Chutney
Honey Lemon Pear Butter
Sweet Pear Caramel
Chunky Pear Preserves with Sage
Red Pear Jam with Lavender
Pear Jam with Chocolate
Pickled Seckel Pears
Maple-Sweetened Apple Butter
Apple Tart Filling
Rosemary Apple Jam
Spiced Apple Half-Moons
Caramelized Shallot Jam
Pickled Garlic Cloves
Pickled Sugar Pumpkin
Pickled Golden Beet Cubes

Fig Jam with Thyme

My friend Albert has a mental map of every publically accessible fig tree within biking distance of his South Philadelphia home. During the season, he checks in with these trees regularly to gather any ripe figs that might be in need of a rescue. Some years, he comes away with many pounds; other years, he finds just a few. Whenever there's a glut, he shares enough with me for a small batch of jam. The herbal flavor of the thyme harmonizes with the figs. You can leave it out if it's not your thing, but I urge you to try it.

MAKES 3 (HALF-PINT/250 ML) JARS

1 dry quart figs (about $1^3/_4$ pounds/790 g)
$1^1/_4$ cups/250 g granulated sugar
2 sprigs fresh thyme (about 3 inches/4.5 cm long)
$1^1/_2$ tablespoons bottled lemon juice

Wash the figs well. Trim away any tough stems and chop each fig into small bits. Place the chopped figs in a small bowl and add the sugar and lemon juice. Stir well. Tuck the thyme sprigs into the macerating figs. Let the fruit rest at room temperature for 30 to 45 minutes, until the sugar is dissolved and the fruit looks syrupy.

When you're ready to cook the jam, prepare a boiling water bath and 3 half-pint/250 ml jars according to the process on page 11. Place 3 lids in a small saucepan of water and bring to a gentle simmer.

To cook, scrape the fruit mixture into a large skillet and place over medium-high heat. Stirring regularly, bring the fruit to a boil and cook until it bubbles and looks quite thick, 10 to 12 minutes. It's done when you pull a spatula through the jam and it doesn't immediately rush in to fill the space you've cleared.

Remove the jam from the heat and funnel into the prepared jars, leaving $1/_2$ inch/12 mm of headspace. Wipe the rims, apply the lids and rings, and process in a boiling water bath for 10 minutes (see pages 11–12).

Pickled Hot Pepper Rings

I am married to a man who can't handle anything spicier than a green pepper. For a girl who likes her food to have a certain level of va-va-voom, this means that I have to do a judicious amount of doctoring at the table to satisfy my taste buds. To that end, I keep bottles of sriracha and sweet chili sauce on the fridge door and, every fall, can up a bunch of pickled hot peppers. I keep the brine unseasoned so they work just as well on sandwiches as they do chopped and stirred into homemade salsa. The other nice thing about this recipe is that comes together in about half an hour. If you're exhausted by your garden and just want to be done with your pepper plants, this approach is a really good answer.

MAKES 3 (HALF-PINT/250 ML) JARS

$1\frac{1}{2}$ cups/360 ml red wine vinegar

$1\frac{1}{2}$ cups/360 ml filtered water

2 tablespoons pickling salt

1 pound/460 g mild hot peppers
(like banana, Mirasol, or Anaheim)

Prepare a small boiling water bath and 3 half-pint/250 ml jars according to the process on page 11. Place 3 lids in a small saucepan of water and bring to the gentle simmer.

Combine the vinegar, water, and salt in a separate saucepan and bring to a boil. When the brine is boiling, add the pepper rings and stir to submerge. As soon as the brine returns to a boil, remove the pot from the heat.

Funnel the peppers into the prepared jars and top with the brine, leaving $\frac{1}{2}$ inch/12 mm of headspace. Tap the jars gently to remove any air bubbles. Add more liquid to return the headspace to $\frac{1}{2}$ inch/12 mm, if necessary. Wipe the rims, apply the lids and rings, and process the jars in a boiling water bath for 10 minutes (see pages 11–12).

The pickled pepper rings are ready to eat within 48 hours.

Note: Save any pickling liquid leftover from this recipe and use it in vinaigrettes or to season sandwiches. The hot peppers will have given it some of their flavor and so it will be just slightly spicy.

Pickled Eggplant with Mint

When you think of a good pickle, eggplant is not necessarily a vegetable that springs immediately to mind. Most of the time, I race to embrace a pickle that is new to me, but I confess, I initially came to the eggplant pickle reluctantly. However, I was proven absolutely wrong with my very first batch. The pickle was zippy and bright with flavor. The texture was tender and without any sign of mushiness. These days, I try to keep a couple of jars on hand for easy holiday party platters. Dressed with drizzle of olive oil and served with a few hunks of feta and bread, it makes an instant appetizer.

MAKES 3 (HALF-PINT/250 ML) JARS

2 cups/480 ml red wine vinegar
1 pound/460 g medium-size purple eggplant,
   peeled and cut into-$\frac{1}{2}$ inch/12 mm cubes
1 tablespoon chopped garlic
$\frac{1}{4}$ cup/30 g mint leaves
1$\frac{1}{2}$ teaspoons pickling salt

Prepare a small boiling water bath and 3 half-pint/250 ml jars according to the process on page 11. Place 3 lids in a small saucepan of water and bring to a gentle simmer.

Pour the vinegar into a medium saucepan and bring to a boil. Once it boils, add the eggplant and simmer for 2 to 3 minutes.

When the time is up, remove the eggplant cubes from the vinegar with a slotted spoon and place them in a bowl. Add the garlic, mint, and salt and stir to combine.

Pack the eggplant, garlic, and mint into the prepared jars and top with the boiling vinegar, leaving $\frac{1}{2}$ inch/12 mm of headspace. Tap the jars gently to remove any air bubbles. Add more liquid to return the headspace to $\frac{1}{2}$ inch/12 mm, if necessary. Wipe the rims, apply the lids and rings, and process the jars in a boiling water bath for 10 minutes (see pages 11–12).

Pickled Crookneck Slices

Every September, I find that I hit something of a squash wall. After eating them steamed, roasted, grilled, panfried, stewed, baked under a cheese sauce, and cooked into a spreadable dip, I cannot bear to look another summer squash in the face. If you find yourself in similar seasonal squash straits, look to the vinegar bottle for a reprieve. Summer squash make wonderfully crisp and flavorful pickles that go really well on sandwiches or chopped and added to salads. I say to use yellow crookneck here, but truly, you can use whatever summer squash is currently haunting you.

MAKES 1 (1-QUART/1-LITER) JAR

1 pound/460 g yellow crookneck squash
1 cup/240 ml distilled white vinegar
1 tablespoon pickling salt
4 lemon slices, divided
1 teaspoon mustard seeds
1 teaspoon dill seeds
1/2 teaspoon black peppercorns

Wash the squash and trim off the ends. Cut the squash into 1/4-inch/6 mm-thick slices. Set aside. In a small saucepan, combine the vinegar, 1 cup of water, and the pickling salt and bring to a boil. Place 2 of the lemon slices in the bottom of a clean 1-quart/1-liter jar. Add the mustard seeds, dill seeds and peppercorns.

Pack the squash slices into the jar, getting them in as tightly as you can. You should be able to get the full pound/460 g of squash into the jar. Slowly pour the hot brine into the jar over the squash, leaving 1/2 inch/12 mm of headspace. Tap the jar gently to remove any air bubbles. Add more liquid to return the headspace to 1/2 inch/12 mm, if necessary. Top with the 2 remaining slices of lemon and apply the lid and ring. Let the jar sit on counter until cool. When the jar is cool, place in the refrigerator. The pickles can be eaten within 48 hours and will keep for up to 2 months.

Note: This pickle cure best when the slices are cut uniformly. For that reason, I always opt for a handheld slicer or mandoline for a job like this one. It makes quick work of the squash and gives you beautiful, even slices.

Red Tomato Pickle

hen it comes to tomatoes, most people go for sauces, salsas, pastes and whole preserved tomatoes. And while I do all those things, I also like to make at least one batch of pickled red tomatoes. Unlike those crunchy pickled green tomatoes you find at delis and gourmet markets, these tomatoes are gorgeously tender and bright with flavor. After a time in the jar with fresh ginger and a bunch of pickling spices, they wind up tasting like an exotic delicacy. I like to squeeze them into bits over homemade pizza dough, cut them into strips to eat with cheese, or simmer them down with a bit of their brine into a quick topper for baguette toasts.

MAKES 3 (HALF-PINT/250 ML) JARS

1 dry quart small, meaty tomatoes (plum, Juliet,
   or San Marzano) (about 2 pounds/910 g)

1 cup/240 ml red wine vinegar

1 cup/240 ml filtered water

1 tablespoon pickling salt

1/3 cup/65 g granulated sugar

1 (1-inch/2.5 cm piece) fresh ginger, thinly sliced, divided

3 teaspoons pickling spice, divided

Bring a medium pot of water to a boil. While it heats, remove the cores from your tomatoes and score the bottoms with a shallow X. Fill a large bowl two-thirds of the way up with ice water.

Working in batches, proceed to blanch all your tomatoes for 1 to 2 minutes, immediately plunging them in the bowl of ice water to stop the cooking. Make sure to give the pot of water a chance to come back up to boiling between batches. If the water isn't hot enough, you will have a hard time removing the skin during peeling.

Once all the tomatoes have been blanched and they are cool enough to touch, remove the skins.

Prepare a boiling water bath and 3 half-pint/250 ml jars according to the process
(continued on next page)

on page 11. Place 3 lids in a small saucepan, cover them with water, and bring to a gentle simmer.

Combine the vinegar, water, salt, sugar, and ginger slices in a large pot and bring to a boil.

Line up your prepared jars and measure 1 teaspoon of pickling spices into the bottom of each jar.

Carefully pack the peeled tomatoes into the jars, taking care not to crush them.

Slowly pour the brine over the tomatoes, leaving $\frac{1}{2}$ inch/12 mm of headspace. Tap the jars gently on a towel-lined countertop to help remove any air bubbles. Use a wooden chopstick or plastic knife to dislodge any trapped bubbles. Add more liquid to return the headspace to $\frac{1}{2}$ inch/12 mm, if necessary. Make sure to include 2 to 3 ginger slices in each jar. Wipe the rims, apply the lids and rings, and process in a boiling water bath for 10 minutes (see pages 11–12). Let these pickles cure for at least a week before eating.

Green Tomato Salsa

The initial spark of inspiration for this salsa came from a fresh version that my mom used to make when I was a teenager. Each October, just before the first freeze, we'd pick the garden bare of any remaining tomatoes, ripe or not, and arrange them on the windowsills in the kitchen and dining room. Right around Thanksgiving, finally fed up with wrinkly, half-ripe tomatoes, my mom would gather the stragglers and make a batch of green tomato salsa. More tart than the version made with ripe tomatoes, it was still delightful when eaten with tortilla chips or poured over scrambled eggs. This cooked version is a little different texturally, but no less delicious.

MAKES 3 (HALF-PINT/250 ML) JARS

1 dry quart firm pale green tomatoes (about 2 pounds/910 g)
1 cup/160 g minced yellow onion (about 1 small onion)

¹⁄₂ cup/100 g seeded and chopped poblano pepper
  (about 1 small pepper)
¹⁄₄ cup/60 ml bottled lime juice
¹⁄₄ cup/50 g granulated sugar
3 garlic cloves, minced
1 teaspoon ground cumin
1 teaspoon finely milled sea salt
¹⁄₄ teaspoon ground coriander
¹⁄₂ teaspoon freshly ground black pepper
Cayenne pepper (optional)

Prepare a boiling water bath and 3 half-pint/250 ml jars according to the process on page 11. Place 3 lids in a small saucepan of water and bring to a gentle simmer.

Core and roughly chop the tomatoes and place them in a medium, heavy-bottomed pot along with the onion, pepper, lime juice, sugar, garlic, cumin, coriander, salt, and black pepper. Bring to a boil and lower the temperature to medium-high. Cook at a simmer for 15 to 20 minutes, until the salsa has reduced by about one-quarter and looks considerably less watery.

When the time is up, remove the pot from the heat and taste the salsa, adjusting the salt and heat levels, as necessary (if you want a hotter salsa, you can add up to 1 teaspoon of cayenne). Funnel the salsa into the prepared jars, leaving ¹⁄₂ inch/12 mm of headspace. Wipe the rims, apply the lids and rings, and process in a boiling water bath for 15 minutes (see pages 11–12).

Pizza Sauce

L ast summer, one of the vendors at my local farmers' market began selling cracked and slightly bruised tomatoes alongside his perfect ones. These seconds were a third of the price of their prettier siblings and just as tasty. Each week, I would buy more than I could possibly eat and so started to play around with little batches of preserves to use up the rest before they started to mold. This pizza sauce became the winning strategy for these tomatoes, as it comes together so quickly. With a ball of homemade dough from the freezer, we're just two steps away from homemade pizza, even on a busy weeknight.

MAKES 2 (HALF-PINT/250 ML) JARS

1 dry quart tomatoes (about 2 pounds/910 g)

1 teaspoon olive oil

1 teaspoon kosher salt

$^1/_2$ teaspoon dried Italian seasoning

$^1/_4$ teaspoon freshly ground black pepper

$^1/_4$ teaspoon citric acid

Prepare a boiling water bath and 2 half-pint/250 ml jars according to the process on page 11. Place 2 lids in a small saucepan of water and bring to a gentle simmer.

Remove the skins from the tomatoes either by blanching them in a pot of boiling water, or with a serrated edge peeler. Core and dice the peeled tomatoes.

Place a large skillet over medium-high heat. Add the oil, tomatoes, salt, Italian seasoning, and pepper. As they heat, use a potato masher or the back of a fork to help the tomato chunks break down into a rough sauce. Bring to a low boil and cook, stirring regularly, until the sauce thickens and reduces by half.

When the sauce is finished cooking, remove it from the heat. Funnel into the prepared jars, leaving $^1/_2$ inch/12 mm of headspace. Wipe the rims, apply the lids and rings, and process in a boiling water bath for 15 minutes (see pages 11–12).

Note: While this sauce can be made with any variety of tomato, choosing a meatier tomato, such as a plum, Roma, or beefsteak, means that your yield will be closer to mine. If you make it with watery tomatoes, bump up the starting weight by half a pound/230 g, to ensure you get the proper yield.

Lacto-Fermented
Green Tomato Pickle

If you've ever had a pickled green tomato from a big tub in a deli, it was lacto-fermented. Instead of relying on acid from an outside source, such as vinegar, you submerge underripe tomatoes in a salt-water brine and let a beneficial bacteria by the name of *Lactobacillus* transmute the natural sugars in the tomatoes into acid. After a few days in the brine, the tomatoes take on a decidedly tart flavor and their skins go from bright green to a more muted shade. It might seem like magic, but it's just the natural process of salt and time.

MAKES 1 (HALF-GALLON/2-LITER) JAR

1 dry quart firm, underripe tomatoes (about 2 pounds/910 g)
2 tablespoons finely milled sea salt
6 garlic cloves, peeled
1 tablespoon black peppercorns
1 tablespoon yellow mustard seeds
1 tablespoon dill seeds
1 teaspoon red chile flakes

Wash the tomatoes well and set to dry. Bring a large kettle of water to a boil and measure 4 cups/1 liter of boiling water into a large measuring cup with a spout. Add the salt and stir to help the salt dissolve. Let the water cool to room temperature.

While the water cools, place the garlic cloves, peppercorns, mustard seeds, dill seeds, and chile flakes in the bottom of a large jar (a wide-mouth half-gallon/2-liter jar is ideal). Pack the tomatoes into the jar and pour in the cooled brine. Tap the jar gently to remove any air bubbles. Cover the jar with a clean cloth and attach with a rubber band.

Set the jar on a small plate and let it sit at a cool room temperature (60° to 68°F/16° to 20°C is ideal) for 5 to 7 days, until the brine tastes quite tangy. At this point, they pickles are ready to eat. Refrigerated, these pickles will keep for 3 to 4 weeks.

Notes: These pickles are best done in late autumn, when the hottest days of summer have passed. If you are struggling to keep the top tomato fully submerged in the brine, fill a very clean quarter-pint/125 ml jar with excess brine and fit it into the mouth of the 1-quart/1-liter jar. Its weight will keep the tomatoes under the brine level.

Quick Pickled Fennel with Orange

When my parents were first married, they bought a great deal of beef from a local farmer for their freezer. Turned out that the cow from which the meat came had liked the taste of wild fennel and so every bite tasted of licorice. After they made it through that order, my mom swore off anything anise-flavored. There's only ever been one thing that's ever been able to tempt her back to the fennel-flavored side and that's this pickle.

MAKES 2 (1-PINT/500 ML) JARS

1 pound/680 g fennel bulbs (2 to 3 small bulbs)
1 tablespoon kosher salt
1 small orange, sliced
$\frac{1}{2}$ teaspoon freshly ground black pepper
1 cup/240 ml cider vinegar

Wash the fennel bulbs and remove the stems. Slice in half and cut out the hard core. Slice paper thin on a mandoline.

Sprinkle the salt over the shaved fennel and toss to combine. Let the fennel sit for at least an hour.

When the time is up, pour the fennel into a colander, rinse lightly, and squeeze to remove the liquid that was produced while it sat with the salt.

Return the fennel to the bowl and toss with the orange slices and pepper.

Pack the fennel mixture into 2 clean 1-pint/500 ml jars and top with the vinegar.

Use a chopstick or the end of a wooden spoon to work the vinegar down into the fennel.

Stash the jar in the fridge and let sit for at least 24 hours before eating.

This quick pickle will keep for at least a month in the refrigerator.

Note: If you think you'll eat through this pickle fairly quickly, you can also pack it into a single 1-quart/1-liter jar. I just find that it lasts a bit longer divided between 2 1-pint/500 ml jars.

Pickled Kohlrabi Matchsticks

If you've never encountered kohlrabi before, it's a nearly round vegetable about the size of a tennis ball. You'll sometimes find it with its series of stems and leaves intact, though many farmers take the time to trim those away before bringing their crop to market or packing them for CSA shares. It comes in a variety of shades of green and purple, is hearty and crunchy, and has a texture resembling that of broccoli stems. Because kohlrabi is in the Brassica family, it's better made as a refrigerator pickle so as to keep that signature cabbage stink from developing during cooking. I like to eat this pickle with salads, sandwiches, or meat dishes.

MAKES 1 (1-QUART/1-LITER) JAR

1 pound/680 g kohlrabi
1 cup/240 ml red wine vinegar
1 cup/240 ml filtered water
1 tablespoon honey
1 tablespoon pickling salt
1 tablespoon grated fresh ginger
1 garlic clove, grated
$\frac{1}{2}$ teaspoon black peppercorns
$\frac{1}{4}$ teaspoon red chile flakes

Clean and trim the kohlrabi bulbs. Using a mandoline slicer or a food processor, slice the kohlrabi into thin sticks and place in a 1-quart/1-liter jar.

Combine the vinegar, water, honey, pickling salt, ginger, garlic, peppercorns, and chile flakes in a medium saucepan and bring to a boil. Lower the heat and cook at a simmer for 10 minutes, to fully infuse spices into the brine.

Once the brine is boiling vigorously, remove it from the heat. Position a small, fine-mesh sieve over the mouth of the jar and carefully pour the brine through the sieve, to catch the spices.

Place a lid on the jar and let the kohlrabi sit until cool.

Once the jar is cool to the touch, refrigerate the pickles. Let them rest for at least 48 hours before eating.

Smooth Tomatillo Simmer Sauce

For years, I was confounded when I'd get tomatillos in my CSA share. Then I discovered this sauce and all those 1-quart containers suddenly had purpose. While it's essentially a salsa, I find that I prefer pouring it over chicken thighs and cooking them over low heat for an hour or two, until the meat shreds and the sauce shimmers. Serve the chicken over cilantro rice or heaped into corn tortillas.

MAKES 2 (HALF-PINT/250 ML) JARS

1 dry quart tomatillos, husked, washed and finely chopped (about $1\frac{1}{2}$ pounds/680 g)

$\frac{1}{4}$ cup/40 g finely chopped yellow onion

2 garlic cloves, crushed

2 tablespoons freshly squeezed lime juice

1 tablespoon minced fresh cilantro

1 teaspoon red chile flakes

1 teaspoon ground cumin

1 teaspoons finely milled sea salt

Prepare a boiling water bath and 2 half-pint/250 ml jars according to the process on page 11. Place 2 lids in a small saucepan of water and bring to a gentle simmer.

Place a large skillet over medium-high heat. Add the tomatillos, onion, garlic, lime juice, cilantro, chile flakes, cumin, and salt, along with $\frac{1}{2}$ cup/120 ml of water. Bring to a low boil and cook, stirring regularly, until the sauce thickens and reduces by one-third, 15 to 20 minutes.

When the sauce looks quite thick, remove it from the heat and scrape it into a blender or food processor. Keep in mind that the sauce is still hot, so take care not to splash yourself. Blend or process until the sauce is smooth. Funnel into the prepared jars, leaving $\frac{1}{2}$ inch/12 mm of headspace. Wipe the rims, apply the lids and rings, and process in a boiling water bath for 15 minutes (see pages 11–12).

Pear Cranberry Chutney

This chutney recipe was born out of necessity. I had a half-pint of fresh cranberries on the counter that were rapidly shriveling and several pears that had developed brown spots overnight. Like most condiments that include cranberry, this chutney plays nicely with leftover roast turkey. Thanks to its pleasing pink tint, it also makes a pretty addition to holiday gift bag and baskets.

MAKES 3 (HALF-PINT/250 ML) JARS

1 pound/460 g Bartlett or Bosc pears, peeled and chopped
1 cup/100 g fresh cranberries
$\frac{1}{2}$ cup/120 ml cider vinegar
$\frac{1}{2}$ cup/115 g packed light brown sugar
$\frac{1}{3}$ cup/60 g raisins
$\frac{1}{3}$ cup/60 g minced red onion
2 teaspoons grated fresh ginger
1 teaspoon finely milled sea salt
$\frac{1}{2}$ teaspoon yellow mustard seeds

Prepare a boiling water bath and 3 half-pint/250 ml jars according to the process on page 11. Place 3 lids in a small saucepan of water and bring to a gentle simmer.

Combine the pears, cranberries, vinegar, brown sugar, raisins, onion, ginger, salt, and mustard seeds in a large, heavy-bottomed pot. Bring to a low boil and then lower the heat to a simmer. Cook over medium heat for 20 to 30 minutes, until the pears melt, the cranberries pop, and the raisins get plump. If the liquid reduces away before the fruit has softened and plumped, add a splash of water to prevent burning.

Once the chutney is thick and there's no sign of runniness, it is finished. Funnel the chutney into the prepared jars, leaving $\frac{1}{2}$ inch/12 mm of headspace. Wipe the rims, apply the lids and rings, and process in a boiling water bath for 10 minutes (see pages 11–12).

Honey Lemon Pear Butter

When I was in my early 20s, I moved to Philadelphia. It has turned out to be a wonderful choice for me, save for the fact that it put 3,000 miles between my parents' home in Oregon. Whenever I'd get excessively homesick, my mom would quickly make a pint jar of honey-sweetened pear butter, wrap it well, and drop it into the mail for me. It would always arrive sealed and in one piece, tasting exactly like home. This is how she made it.

MAKES 2 (HALF-PINT/250 ML) JARS

2 pounds/910 g Bartlett pears (5 to 6 pears)
$^1/_3$ cup/120 g honey
1 teaspoon ground cinnamon
Zest and juice of 1 lemon

Prepare a boiling water bath and 2 half-pint/250 ml jars according to the process on page 11. Place 2 lids in a small saucepan of water and bring to a gentle simmer.

Wash, core, and quarter the pears. Place the pears in a medium saucepan with 2 tablespoons of water. Set the pan over medium-low heat and simmer for 10 to 15 minutes, until the pears are quite smooth.

Scrape the softened pears into the carafe of a blender and purée until the skins disappear and the flesh is quite tender. Return the purée to the saucepan and place over low heat.

Cook, stirring regularly, for 45 to 55 minutes, until the pear purée has thickened a great deal and sits up tall in the bowl of a spoon. If it's not done, it will run to the edges of the spoon and will be no higher than the rim.

Add the honey, lemon juice and zest, and cinnamon. Taste and adjust the sweet and tart levels.

Remove the butter from the heat and funnel into the prepared jars, leaving $^1/_2$ inch/12 mm of headspace. Wipe the rims, apply the lids and rings, and process in a boiling water bath for 10 minutes (see pages 11–12).

Sweet Pear Caramel

learned that canning fruit-based caramel sauces was possible, thanks to an article posted to *Gilt Taste* in early 2012. It offered a recipe using strawberry purée, but once I had the formula in hand, I tried it with every variety of fruit that I could find. I came to like this version best because the mellow flavor of the pears seemed to harmonize with the toasted sugar instead of fighting it. Like all caramel sauces, this one is ridiculous over vanilla ice cream.

MAKES 2 (HALF-PINT/250 ML) JARS

1 pound/460 g ripe pears, Bartlett, Bosc, or Anjou
½ teaspoon finely milled sea salt
1½ cup/300 g granulated sugar

Prepare a boiling water bath and 2 half-pint/250 ml jars according to the process on page 11. Place 2 lids in a small saucepan of water and bring to a gentle simmer.

Peel, core and chop the pears. Place them in a blender with the salt and 2 tablespoons of water. Purée until smooth. You should have about 1½ cups/370 g of pear purée.

Combine the sugar with ¾ cup/180 ml of water in a saucepan. Place over medium-high heat and simmer for 15 to 20 minutes, until the sugar reaches 350°F180°C and darkens to the color of a tarnished copper penny. Do not stir the cooking syrup; instead, holding the handle of the pot, gently swirl it to move things around.

Once the syrup has reached 350°F/180°C, remove the pot from the heat and stir in the pear purée. It will bubble, spatter, and appear to seize up, so take care. Stir the purée into the sugar until it is a smooth sauce and return the pot to the heat. Continue stirring and cooking until the pear caramel sauce reaches 218°F/104°C.

Remove the caramel from the heat and funnel into the prepared jars, leaving ½ inch/12 mm of headspace. Wipe the rims, apply the lids and rings, and process in a boiling water bath for 10 minutes (see pages 11–12).

Note: If your caramel sauce gets too firm to drizzle easily, place the jar in a pan of lukewarm water and slowly bring it up to a simmer, until the sauce relaxes enough to be pourable.

Chunky Pear
Preserves with Sage

This preserve falls somewhere between a jam and preserved pear halves in syrup. Peeled and roughly chopped, these pears are best stirred into Greek yogurt or heaped onto a salad of baby lettuces. The sage gives them a pleasingly herbaceous bite that balances the sweetness of the syrup. If sage isn't your thing, you can also substitute rosemary or lavender, or simply leave the herbs out entirely. When all the pears are gone from the jar, drizzle the remaining syrup into sparkling water for refreshing, bubbly beverage.

MAKES 3 (HALF-PINT/250 ML) JARS

1 pound/460 g pears (about 3 good-size pears)
$\frac{1}{2}$ cup/170 g honey
20 fresh sage leaves
Juice of 1 lemon

Prepare a boiling water bath and 3 half-pint/250 ml jars according to the process on page 11. Place 3 lids in a small saucepan of water and bring to a gentle simmer.

In a medium saucepan, combine the honey with $1\frac{1}{2}$ cups/360 ml of water, the sage leaves, and lemon juice and bring to a boil. While it heats, peel, core, and roughly chop the pears.

Slip the pears into the hot syrup and cook for 2 to 3 minutes, just until it returns to a boil.

Funnel the pears into the prepared jars and top with the hot syrup, skimming out the spent sage leaves as you pour, leaving $\frac{1}{2}$ inch/12 mm of headspace. Tap the jars gently to remove any air bubbles. Add more liquid to return the headspace to $\frac{1}{2}$ inch/12 mm, if necessary. Wipe the rims, apply the lids and bands, and process the jars in a boiling water bath for 10 minutes (see pages 11–12).

Red Pear Jam with Lavender

I find that red pears don't taste markedly different from their yellow and brown cousins. However, I call for them in this recipe because, when cooked, their bright skins bleed out some of their color, leaving you with a rosy-colored jam shot through with slips of darker pink that tastes just slightly of flowers, thanks to the lavender buds. It is decidedly girly and should be served at tea parties, preferably with cream scones or toast points.

MAKES 2 (HALF-PINT/250 ML) JARS

1$\frac{1}{2}$ pounds/680 g red pears (about 3$\frac{1}{2}$ cups chopped)
1 cup/200 g granulated sugar
Juice from $\frac{1}{2}$ lemon
1 tablespoon food-grade lavender buds

Core the pears and chop into a small dice. Place in a small bowl and add the sugar and lemon juice. Stir to combine. Place the lavender buds into a small spice bag or tie them up tightly in a length of cheesecloth. Tuck the lavender packet into the bowl with the pears and sugar. Let the fruit sit on the counter for 15 to 30 minutes, until the sugar is mostly dissolved and the pears have released some of their juice.

Prepare a boiling water bath and 2 half-pint/250 ml jars according to the process on page 11. Place 2 lids in a small saucepan of water and bring to a gentle simmer.

To cook, pour the fruit in to a large skillet and place over medium-high heat. Stirring regularly, bring the fruit to a boil and cook until it has thickened into jam, 10 to 12 minutes. It's done when you pull a spatula through the jam and it doesn't immediately rush in to fill the space you've cleared.

Remove the jam from the heat and fish out the lavender packet. Funnel into the prepared jars, leaving $\frac{1}{2}$ inch/12 mm of headspace. Wipe the rims, apply the lids and rings, and process in a boiling water bath for 10 minutes (see pages 11–12).

Pear Jam with Chocolate

The way I see it, there are two kinds of jam in the world. There's your workaday jams, the ones that you spread on sandwiches, shake into vinaigrettes, or use to sweeten bowls of plain yogurt. And then there are the special-occasion jams. Those are the ones that you give as gifts, pull out for special brunches, or savor on holiday mornings. For me, this jam falls into that latter category, particularly when spread on toasted challah. Many thanks to Mary Tregalla and her book *Notes from the Jam Cupboard*, for the initial inspiration.

MAKES 2 (HALF-PINT/250 ML) JARS

$1\frac{1}{2}$ pounds/680 g ripe, thin-skinned pears
   (Bartlett, Bosc, or Anjou)
$\frac{3}{4}$ cup/150 g granulated sugar
Juice of $\frac{1}{2}$ lemon
1 tablespoon unsweetened cocoa powder

Core the pears and chop into a small dice. Place in a small bowl and add the sugar and lemon juice. Stir well to integrate the sugar and break up the pears a little.

When you're ready to cook the jam, prepare a boiling water bath and 2 half-pint/250 ml jars according to the process on page 11. Place 2 lids in a small saucepan of water and bring to a gentle simmer.

To cook, scrape the pears into a large skillet and place over medium-high heat. Stirring regularly, bring the fruit to a boil and cook until it bubbles and looks quite thick, 8 to 10 minutes. It's done when you pull a spatula through the jam and it doesn't immediately rush in to fill the space you've cleared.

Remove the jam from heat and stir in the cocoa powder. When it's fully integrated, funnel the jam into the prepared jars, leaving $\frac{1}{2}$ inch/12 mm of headspace. Wipe the rims, apply the lids and rings, and process in a boiling water bath for 10 minutes (see pages 11–12).

Pickled Seckel Pears

I discovered tiny Seckel pears sometime in late 2002. If you haven't seen one before, it looks like a small, burnished Bosc. They have fresh, crisp flavor with just a hint of natural spice and happen to also to be downright adorable. Seckels are long prized by canners for their firm flesh and manageable size and I find that I like them best when they've been gently pickled. Because they come into season in late September and early October, you can put them up after the frenzy of the summer canning season has come to an end. Packed into a small basket with a wedge of sharp Cheddar cheese and a bag of homemade crackers, they make a winning holiday gift.

MAKES 2 (1-PINT/500 ML) JARS

1 dry quart Seckel pears (about $1\frac{1}{2}$ pounds/680 g)
1 cup/240 ml cider vinegar
$\frac{1}{3}$ cup/65 g granulated sugar
1 teaspoon pickling salt
1 cinnamon stick, broken in half, divided
6 whole cloves, divided

Prepare a small boiling water bath and 2 (1-pint/500 ml) jars according to the process on page 11. Place 2 lids in a small saucepan and bring to a gentle simmer.

In a small pan, combine the cider vinegar, 1 cup/240 ml of water and the sugar and salt and bring to a boil.

While the brine heats, wash the pears. Halve and remove the seeds (a small melon baller does this latter task well).

Divide the cinnamon stick halves and cloves between the prepared jars and tightly pack the pear halves into the jars, cut-side down.

Pour the hot brine over the pears, leaving $\frac{1}{2}$ inch/12 mm of headspace. Tap the jars gently to remove any air bubbles. Add more liquid to return the headspace to $\frac{1}{2}$ inch/12 mm, if necessary. Wipe the rims, apply the lids and bands, and process the jars in a boiling water bath for 15 minutes (see pages 11–12).

Note: If you can't find Seckel pears, similarly sized Forelle pears are a good substitute.

Maple-Sweetened Apple Butter

When Scott and I were on our honeymoon, two mornings in a row we ate breakfast at a backwoods joint in Vermont. The pancakes were fluffy, the coffee was strong, and the maple syrup had been tapped and cooked down on-site. Both days, I ordered the special, which was a short stack of pancakes with buttery, griddle-seared apple slices on top. This apple butter reminds me of those happy days.

**MAKES 2 (HALF-PINT/250 ML) JARS
AND 1 (QUARTER-PINT/125 ML) JAR**

2 pounds/910 g apples (5 to 6 apples)
$^1/_3$ cup/80 ml grade B maple syrup
$^3/_4$ teaspoon ground cinnamon
$^1/_4$ teaspoon freshly grated nutmeg
Juice of $^1/_2$ lemon

Prepare a boiling water bath, 2 half-pint/250 ml jars and 1 quarter-pint/125 ml jar according to the process on page 11. Place 3 lids in a small saucepan of water and bring to a gentle simmer.

Wash, core, and quarter the apples. Place the apples and 2 tablespoons of water in a medium saucepan. Set the pan over medium-low heat and simmer for 10 to 15 minutes, until the fruit is quite tender.

Scrape the softened apples into the carafe of a blender and purée until the skins disappear and the flesh is quite smooth. Return the purée to the saucepan and place over low heat.

Cook, stirring regularly, for 20 to 30 minutes, until the apple purée has thickened a great deal and sits up tall in the bowl of a spoon. If it's not done, it will run to the edges of the spoon and will be no higher than the rim.

Add the maple syrup, spices, and lemon juice. Taste and adjust the sweet and tart levels.

Remove the butter from the heat and funnel into the prepared jars, leaving $^1/_2$ inch/12 mm of headspace. Wipe the rims, apply the lids and rings, and process in a boiling water bath for 10 minutes (see pages 11–12).

Apple Tart Filling

Eugenia Bone is one of my canning heroes. Her lovely book, *Well Preserved*, is one I reference regularly and deserves a spot every canner's bookshelf. This recipe is adapted from her Spiced Apples and is perfect as a filling for tarts or turnovers. On chilly mornings, a scoop of these apples stirred into a bowl of steamy oatmeal makes for a wholesome and tasty start to the day.

MAKES 2 (HALF-PINT/250 ML) JARS

1$\frac{1}{2}$ pounds/680 g apples (use something tart and crisp)
3 tablespoons granulated sugar, divided
$\frac{1}{2}$ teaspoon ground cinnamon
$\frac{1}{4}$ teaspoon freshly grated nutmeg
$\frac{1}{8}$ teaspoon ground cloves
$\frac{1}{2}$ teaspoon citric acid, divided

Prepare a boiling water bath and 2 half-pint/250 ml jars according to the process on page 11. Place 2 lids in a small saucepan of water and bring to a gentle simmer.

Line a sieve or colander with a thin kitchen towel and place it over a large bowl. Grate the apples into the lined sieve. Add 1 tablespoon of the sugar and toss gently to combine. Let the apples sit for 10 minutes, until they are beginning to look juicy.

Gather up the sides of the towel and squeeze out some of the juice from the apples. You should yield $\frac{1}{2}$ to $\frac{3}{4}$ cup/120 to 180 ml.

Measure half of reserved apple juice into a medium saucepan and add the remaining 2 tablespoons of sugar, along with the spices.

Once the sugar has dissolved, add the apples. Cook for 5 to 6 minutes, until the apple shreds have broken down a little and reabsorbed the spiced juice.

Divide the citric acid between the 2 half-pint/250 ml jars and pack the hot apple shreds into the jars, leaving $\frac{3}{4}$ inch/2 mm of headspace. Wipe the rims, apply the lids and rings, and process in a boiling water bath for 25 minutes (see pages 11–12). When the time is up, remove the pot from the heat and let the jars stand in the warm water for an additional 5 minutes. This extra time improves the chances that the apples won't siphon out of the jars.

Note: Most products don't need that extra 5 minutes in the pot off the heat, but the thickness of this apple filling benefits from the extra time.

Easy Dinner

When I think back to the many family dinners of my childhood, I see a white plate sitting on a round oak table. On the plate is a small mound of brown rice, a pile of steamed and buttered green beans, and an oven-roasted chicken leg. Sometimes in this memory, a few wedges of baked sweet potato take the place of the rice, and broccoli subs in for the beans, but the baked chicken leg is ever present.

My mom has always been the day-to-day cook in my family (my dad handles weekend breakfasts and special occasions). When approaching meal planning, her priorities have always been to make things that are relatively easy, healthy, inexpensive, and good. The formula of a whole grain (or vitamin-rich starch), green vegetable, and protein checked all the boxes and, on most nights, resulted in happy eaters.

To ensure that we not become bored with the chicken leg (her favorite for its flavor and quick cooking time), my mom did her best to change up her treatment of this portion of the bird. Some nights, they would be marinated in sweet teriyaki sauce. Other times, she'd stir up a combination of grainy mustard and honey and paint the sauce on the legs. However, my favorite version always involved a generous dollop of either apricot or peach jam.

My mom would line an old rectangular baking tin with aluminum foil to make for easier cleanup. Then, she'd arrange the chicken legs in the pan so that they fit together neatly. The required amount of jam to dress the chicken pieces would be spooned into a bowl, to prevent any cross-contamination, and then smeared atop each piece. Knowing that we'd eat more if there was a dipping action involved, my parents always served us an extra little puddle of jam on the side.

Making jam-glazed chicken parts (obviously, you're not actually limited to using legs for this treatment) is incredibly simple and is still one of my favorite ways to make chicken for a speedy weeknight meal. These days, I like to add just a touch of vinegar and a bit of grated ginger to the jam, for a little tangy heat, but the general approach is still the same, delicious one I grew up eating.

Jam-Glazed Chicken Legs

When you pick out jam to use in this dish, reach for a jar that has a firmer set. Because you're going to stir a little vinegar into it, you don't want to use a runny batch.

SERVES 4

1 ½ to 2 pounds/680 to 910 g chicken legs
  (depending on your appetites)
½ cup/160 g apricot or peach jam
1 tablespoon rice vinegar
2 teaspoons grated fresh ginger
1 garlic clove, grated
1 teaspoon sea salt
½ teaspoon freshly ground black pepper

Preheat the oven to 350°F/180°C. Line a baking pan with aluminum foil. Pat the chicken legs dry with paper towels to ensure good jam adherence and arrange the legs in the pan.

In a small bowl, combine the jam, vinegar, ginger, and garlic. Season the chicken, divide the spiked jam among the legs, and use the back of the spoon to spread it evenly.

Cover the pan with foil and place it in the oven. Bake for 40 minutes, then remove the foil and continue to cook for another 10 to 15 minutes, until the tops of the chicken pieces bubble and brown, and an instant-read thermometer shows an internal temperature of at least 165°F/74°C.

Remove the glazed chicken from the oven and let it rest for 5 minutes before serving.

Rosemary Apple Jam

A few years back, I spent a restless two weeks in Austin, Texas, waiting for my sister to give birth to her first child. While I was down South, I spent some time with Stephanie McClenny. She owns Confituras, an Austin-based jam company that sells jams and jellies made in small, hand-tended batches. Before I left town, she gave me a jar of her rosemary-infused apple jam. It was delicious, and when I got home, I set about trying to make my own version. The addition of rosemary makes this jam a particularly good choice for glazing chicken and pork.

MAKES 2 (HALF-PINT/250 ML) JARS

$1\frac{1}{2}$ pounds/680 g apples (about 4 cups chopped)
4 sprigs rosemary, divided
$\frac{1}{2}$ cup/100 g granulated sugar
Zest and juice of $\frac{1}{2}$ lemon

Peel, core, and dice the apples. Place in a saucepan with 2 tablespoons of water and 3 rosemary sprigs. Cover the pan, place over medium heat, and bring to a simmer. Cook until the apples are tender like applesauce and can be mashed with the tines of a fork, 10 to 20 minutes.

Prepare a boiling water bath and 2 half-pint/250 ml jars according to the process on page 11. Place 2 lids in a small saucepan of water and bring to a gentle simmer.

To cook, pour the fruit into a large skillet. Off the heat, stir the sugar into the apples and taste. If you're happy with the level of rosemary flavor, set the final sprig of rosemary aside and set the skillet over medium-high heat. If you'd like to infuse a little more rosemary essence, drop the remaining sprig into the jam. After tasting, stir in the lemon juice.

Stirring regularly, bring the fruit to a boil and cook until it bubbles madly and appears to thicken, 8 to 10 minutes. It's done when you pull a spatula through the jam and it doesn't immediately rush in to fill the space you've cleared.

Remove the jam from the heat and funnel into the prepared jars, leaving $\frac{1}{2}$ inch/12 mm of headspace. Wipe the rims, apply the lids and rings, and process in a boiling water bath for 10 minutes (see pages 11–12).

Spiced Apple Half-Moons

This is my take on the classic spiced apple rings with which many an old-time canner will be familiar. The traditional recipe instructs canners to add either red hot cinnamon candies or cinnamon extract and food coloring for flavor and looks. My version uses a more modern array of spices and skips the lurid red dye entirely. I like to float these lightly pickled slices in mugs of mulled cider during the chilly months of winter.

MAKES 3 (HALF-PINT/250 ML) JARS

1 tablespoon bottled lemon juice

1 dry quart firm tart apples (about 1½ pounds/680 g)

2 cups/400 g granulated sugar

¼ cup/60 ml cider vinegar

1 teaspoon whole cloves

½ teaspoon black peppercorns

1 cinnamon stick

1 star anise

Prepare a boiling water bath and 3 half-pint/250 ml jars according to the process on page 11. Place 3 lids in a small saucepan of water and bring to a gentle simmer.

Fill a nonreactive bowl with water and add the lemon juice. Peel, core, and slice the apples in half. Once sliced, place in the lemon water.

In a medium saucepan, combine the sugar, vinegar, and 1½ cups/360 ml of water. Bundle the cloves, black peppercorns, cinnamon stick, and star anise in a length of cheesecloth or a muslin spice bag and add it to the pan. Cook for 3 to 4 minutes, stirring constantly.

Remove the apples from the lemon water and place them in the hot syrup. Stir to coat and then cook for 5 minutes, until the apples begin to soften slightly.

When the time is up, remove the pot from the heat and pull out the spice bundle. Funnel the apple segments into the prepared jars, leaving ½ inch/12 mm of headspace. Wipe the rims, apply the lids and rings, and process in a boiling water bath for 10 minutes (see pages 11–12).

Caramelized Shallot Jam

I used to be intimated by shallots. I assumed they were fussy, fancy, and far too high and mighty for my basic home cooking. Why use shallots when onions would do? That all changed when a friend served me a slice of her homemade pizza topped with some caramelized shallots, fresh mozzarella, and a drizzle of good balsamic. It was slightly delicate and bursting with flavor. I was instantly converted. I regularly use shallots and like to keep a jar of this savory jam in the fridge for slathering on toasted baguette rounds or homemade flatbread, or alongside a variety of cheeses.

MAKES 2 (HALF-PINT/250 ML) JARS

1 pound/460 g shallots
2 tablespoons unsalted butter
2 teaspoons finely milled sea salt
2 tablespoons granulated sugar
1 tablespoon minced fresh rosemary
$\frac{1}{4}$ teaspoon freshly ground black pepper
$\frac{2}{3}$ cup/160 ml balsamic vinegar

Peel the shallots and slice them thinly.

Melt the butter in a large skillet over low heat. When it foams, add the sliced shallots. Stir the shallots to coat them with the butter. Add the salt and sugar and stir again.

Cook the shallots, stirring regularly, until they are deeply browned and reduced in volume by at least half. This should take between 35 and 40 minutes. If they begin to stick during cooking, add a splash of water to prevent burning and encourage softening.

Once the shallots are greatly reduced, raise the heat to medium-high and add the rosemary, pepper, and vinegar.

Cook the shallots for 6 to 8 minutes over medium-high heat, stirring constantly, until the vinegar has reduced and the shallots don't look at all watery.

When it's finished cooking, divide the jam between 2 clean half-pint/250 ml jars. It will keep for 3 to 4 weeks in the refrigerator. For longer storage, this jam can be frozen for up to 6 months.

Pickled Garlic Cloves

When I was younger, I thought the very best part of a jar of pickles was when you got to the end and could eat the garlic cloves at the bottom. It was a very good day when I realized that I didn't have to finish a jar to get to the garlic clove but could instead make whole jars of pickled garlic. In addition to eating them whole, I often smash a few cloves into paste and spread it on sandwiches. They also raise homemade mayonnaise to a new level.

MAKES 3 (HALF-PINT/250 ML) JARS

1 pound/460 g fresh garlic, peeled
2 cups/480 ml red wine vinegar
1 tablespoon pickling salt
3 teaspoons mixed pickling spice, divided

Prepare a small boiling water bath and 3 half-pint/250 ml jars according to the process on page 11. Place 3 lids in a small saucepan of water and bring to the gentle simmer.

Combine the vinegar and salt in a separate saucepan and bring to a boil.

Divide the pickling spice evenly among the three jars. Pack the garlic cloves into the jars over the spices. Pour the hot brine over the garlic cloves, leaving ½ inch/12 mm of headspace. Tap the jars gently to remove any air bubbles. Add more liquid to return the headspace to ½ inch/12 mm, if necessary. Wipe the rims, apply the lids and rings, and process the jars in a boiling water bath for 10 minutes (see pages 11–12).

Let the pickled garlic cure for at least a week before eating.

Note: There are many techniques for peeling a lot of garlic quickly. To my mind, the easiest way is to break apart the heads by pressing on them firmly with the heel of your hand and blanch the separated cloves in a pot of boiling water for 1 minute. When they come out of the hot water, shock them in an ice bath. The papery peels should pull away easily after that. I also find that a quick dip in hot water takes away some of the garlic's natural bitterness, which in my opinion is a plus.

Pickled Sugar Pumpkin

Come autumn, the world goes a little bit pumpkin crazy. Between pumpkin lattes, muffins, doughnuts, and pie, no one can be blamed for feeling a little pumpkin-ed out. Therefore, I entreat you, before you reach your pumpkin saturation point, make these pumpkin pickles. They are sweet, squashy, dense, and tangy. If you are someone who likes a good pumpkin curry, these are most definitely up your alley. These pickles make a really fun addition to a Thanksgiving cheese plate or dessert spread. I also like tumbling them into a salad of baby arugula, crumbled goat cheese, and some of the Caramelized Shallot Jam on page 000. It's my favorite fall potluck dish.

MAKES 2 (HALF-PINT/250 ML) JARS

1 small sugar pumpkin (about 1$\frac{1}{2}$ pounds/680 g)
1$\frac{1}{2}$ cups/360 ml cider vinegar
1 cup/240 ml filtered water
1 cup/200 g granulated sugar
10 black peppercorns
8 whole cloves
5 allspice berries
1 cinnamon stick, crushed
1 bay leaf

Prepare a small boiling water bath and 2 half-pint/250 ml jars according to the process on page 11. Place 2 lids in a small saucepan and bring to a gentle simmer.

Peel the pumpkin, remove the inner seeds and strings, and cut into $\frac{1}{2}$-inch/2 mm dice.

In a medium pot, combine the vinegar, water, and sugar. Heat to dissolve the sugar.

Place the peppercorns, cloves, allspice berries, crushed cinnamon sticks, and bay leaf in a muslin spice bag or tie them tightly in a length of cheesecloth.

Add the pumpkin chunks and spice bag to the syrup. Bring to a boil and then lower the heat to a simmer.

(continued on next page)

Cook the pumpkin in the pickling liquid for 30 to 40 minutes, until the chunks are translucent and fork-tender.

When the pumpkin is done cooking, ladle it into the prepared jars. Cover with the brine, leaving $\frac{1}{2}$ inch/12 mm of headspace. Wipe the rims, apply the lids and rings, and process in a boiling water bath for 20 minutes (see pages 11–12).

Let the pickles cure for at least 2 weeks prior to eating.

Note: You may have heard that it is unsafe to can pumpkin in a boiling water bath canner and in most cases that is true. Pumpkin products, such as butter and purée, are both low in acid (which is necessary for safe canning) and very dense. However, when you can a pumpkin pickle, it is suspended in vinegar brine, which provides the acidity, and the pumpkin is left in chunks (no worries about density!).

Pickled Golden Beet Cubes

I have a dear friend who won't cook beets at home because they make a mess in the kitchen. While it's true that red beets have a tendency to bleed deep magenta when peeled and sliced, this doesn't mean you have to give them up entirely. Opting instead for golden beets means that you get all that sweet, earthy flavor without the same staining your countertops and cutting boards.

MAKES 3 (HALF-PINT/250 ML) JARS

1 pound/460 g golden beets, boiled until fork-tender,
   then peeled and cubed
1 $\frac{1}{2}$ cups/360 ml cider vinegar
$\frac{1}{2}$ cup/120 ml filtered water
1 tablespoon finely milled sea salt
3 teaspoons pickling spice, divided

Prepare a boiling water bath and 3 half-pint/250 ml jars according to the process on page 11. Place 3 lids in a small saucepan and bring to a gentle simmer.

Combine the vinegar, water, and salt in a small saucepan, bring to a boil, and add the beets. Place 1 teaspoon of the pickling spice in each of the prepared jars. Spoon the beets into the jars and then top with hot brine, leaving $\frac{1}{2}$ inch/12 mm of headspace. Tap the jars gently to remove any air bubbles. Add more liquid to return the headspace to $\frac{1}{2}$ inch/12 mm, if necessary. Wipe the rims, apply the lids and rings, and process the jars in a boiling water bath for 10 minutes (see pages 11–12).

Let the pickled beets cure for at least 1 week prior to eating.

Note: Golden beets will sometimes fade over time and can take on a slightly grayish hue. When this happens, they are still perfectly edible, just not quite as beautiful. Keeping them stored out of direct light will slow their fade. If you don't have your own pickling spice blend on hand, I like the one sold by Penzeys.

Winter

RECIPES

My parents have a lovely friend named Tess who
hosts a yearly solstice party. The invitation always asks that guests bring a
potluck dish, a contribution to the local food bank, and candles in sturdy
holders. When everyone has been fed and faces are warm from wine and
conversation, Tess rolls up the rugs, turns out the lights, and leads a candle-
lighting ceremony to welcome the cold, dark days. One by one, we light our
candles and share an image of winter. There are always mentions of snowy
mountain tops and the warmth of hand-knit woolens. When my turn comes,
I always reference the summer and fall I spent canning, and the joy I feel at
finally opening those carefully preserved jars.

The only flaw in the words I share is that I give people the idea that I believe
canning is only something that can be done for part of the year. And while I do
like to go a little easier on myself come December, January, and February,
there's still so much that can be made during the colder months. Root vegetables get sweeter after the first frost and fresh citrus starts arriving from California, Texas, and Florida. So many of us have caches of cranberries in our
freezers, left over from the holidays, and there are always apples and pears
from cold storage at local markets. Cruciferous vegetables, such as cauliflower
and cabbage, are also in abundance and make excellent pickles. And when
warmer weather comes back around, those jars of Meyer lemon marmalade go
so well drizzled over a slice of summer pound cake.

Savory Quince Preserves

Quince Slices in Chai Tea Syrup

Persimmon Chutney

Cranberry Ginger Syrup

Spicy Apple Cider and Mustard Glaze

Winter Fruit Mostarda

Dilled Carrot Spears

Carrot Relish

Spicy Pickled Cauliflower

Pickled Oyster Mushrooms

Lemon, Parsley, and Garlic Salt

Butternut Squash Butter

Caramelized Onion Spread with Sage

Single-Quart Sauerkraut

Lavender Lemon Marmalade

Salt-Preserved Meyer Lemons

Strawberry Meyer Lemon Marmalade

Caramelized Meyer Lemon Syrup

Candied Meyer Lemon Slices in Syrup

Kumquat Marmalade

Pickled Kumquats

Orange Cardamom Curd

Savory Quince Preserves

T his recipe is adapted from one that my friend Janet makes every fall. She initially shared it on her blog, *A Raisin and a Porpoise*, and after my first bite, it became one of my early winter staples. The secret about making is that you roast the quinces before you chop them, which softens the tough flesh and makes them easy to slice. It's particularly good with whole-grain bread and aged Cheddar cheese.

MAKES 3 (HALF-PINT/250 ML) JARS

1 dry quart quinces (about 1$\frac{1}{2}$ pounds/680 g)
$\frac{1}{2}$ cup/100 g granulated sugar
Juice of 1 lemon
2 teaspoons grated fresh ginger
$\frac{1}{4}$ teaspoon ground cumin
$\frac{1}{4}$ teaspoon ground coriander
$\frac{1}{8}$ teaspoon cayenne pepper

Preheat the oven to 350°F/180°C.

Rinse the quinces well, making sure to rub off any surface fuzz. Place them whole in a baking dish and bake for 25 to 30 minutes, until they are light brown and fork-tender.

Once the quinces are cool enough to handle, quarter the quinces and remove the cores and skins. Chop the quince flesh into chunks.

Prepare a boiling water bath and 3 half-pint/250 ml jars according to the process on page 11. Place 3 lids in a small saucepan of water and bring to a gentle simmer.

Place the quince pieces, sugar, lemon juice, and $\frac{1}{2}$ cup of water in a heavy, nonreactive pot. Bring to a simmer, stirring frequently. Cook until the quince pieces break down and thicken (add a splash more water if things they haven't softened sufficiently).

When the quince is soft, use a potato masher to break it up. Then add the ginger, cumin, coriander, and cayenne and stir to combine. Simmer for a few minutes, taste, and adjust the flavor balance (add more lemon juice, sugar, or spices).

When the preserves have a spreadable texture and taste good to you, remove the pot from the heat. Funnel the preserves into the prepared jars, leaving $\frac{1}{2}$ inch/12 mm headspace, wipe the rims, apply the lids and rings, and process in a boiling water bath for 10 minutes (see pages 11–12).

Quince Slices in Chai Tea Syrup

My friend Alexis is a tea writer and enthusiast. She is always encouraging me to find ways to incorporate tea into my preserves. We teamed up to create this recipe and were both tickled with the result. The slivers of quince are tender, slightly rosy in color and infused with the flavor of the black chai-spiced tea. We ate the finished product over yogurt and wished we had slices of gingerbread to soak up the syrup. Yum.

MAKES 3 (HALF-PINT/250 ML) JARS

1½ pounds/680 g quinces (3 to 4 quinces)
1½ cups/300 g granulated sugar
2 tablespoons loose chai-spiced black tea, or four chai tea bags

Prepare a boiling water bath and 3 half-pint/250 ml jars according to the process on page 11. Place 3 lids in a small saucepan of water and bring to a gentle simmer.

Peel, core, and slice the quinces into thin slivers. In a medium saucepan, combine the sugar with 1½ cups/360 ml of water. If using the loose tea, tuck it into a paper filter or a large stainless-steel tea ball and add it to the pot. Finally, slide the quince slices into the pot and bring the whole thing to a boil. Cook at a low boil for 15 to 20 minutes. Taste the syrup and if the level of chai flavor is to your liking, remove the tea bags or ball. Continue to cook until the quince goes slightly translucent and is tender when pierced with a fork.

When the quince is done to your liking, remove the saucepan from the heat. Using a slotted spoon, transfer the quince to the prepared jars. Return the syrup to the stove, bring it back up to a boil and cook for 10 to 15 minutes, until it reaches 218°F/104°C, has reduced, and looks quite thick (you'll need about 1 cup/240 ml of syrup to top off the jars). Ladle the thickened syrup over the fruit, leaving ½ inch/12 mm of headspace. Tap the jars gently to remove any air bubbles. Add more liquid to return the headspace to ½ inch/12 mm, if necessary. Wipe the rims, apply the lids and rings, and process in a boiling water bath for 10 minutes (see pages 11–12).

Persimmon Chutney

Each December, I go back to Portland, Oregon, for the holidays. One year, my mom and I were out walking and stopped to admire a tree hanging heavy with persimmons in a neighbor's yard. As we stood there, the owner came out of the house and handed us a bag containing half a dozen plump, brilliant orange persimmons. He said, "I could tell you wanted some and we have more than plenty to share." We said our thanks, took the fruit home, and this chutney was born.

MAKES 2 (HALF-PINT/250 ML) JARS

1 dry quart Fuyu persimmons (about $1^{1}/_{2}$ pounds/680 g)

2 small shallots, chopped

$^{1}/_{2}$ cup/120 ml cider vinegar

$^{2}/_{3}$ cup/150 g packed light brown sugar

$^{1}/_{2}$ cup/85 g raisins

1 teaspoon finely milled sea salt

$^{1}/_{2}$ teaspoon ground cloves

$^{1}/_{4}$ teaspoon red chile flakes

Prepare a boiling water bath and 2 half-pint/250 ml jars according to the process on page 11. Place 2 lids in a small saucepan of water and bring to a gentle simmer.

Core and finely chop the persimmons. Combine them in a large, heavy-bottomed pot with the shallots, vinegar, brown sugar, and raisins. Bring to a simmer and cook over medium heat for 20 to 30 minutes, until the persimmon begins to break down and the raisins get plump.

When the persimmon is tender, add the salt, cloves, and chile flakes. Stir to combine and cook to integrate the spices.

Once the chutney is thick and there's no sign of runniness, it is finished. Funnel the chutney into the prepared jars, leaving $^{1}/_{2}$ inch/12 mm of headspace. Wipe the rims, apply the lids and rings, and process in a boiling water bath for 10 minutes (see pages 11–12).

Note: Make sure to use Fuyu persimmons in this recipe. They have flat bottoms and are sweet and flavorful even when firm. Hachiya persimmons have a pointy bottom and are tart and astringent until absolutely ripe: then they're too soft for chutney.

Cranberry Ginger Syrup

have a habit of stocking up on cranberries when they go on sale around Thanksgiving. I tuck the bags into a larger resealable plastic bag and stash them in the freezer for later. When "later" eventually arrives (most often when the freezer is bursting and something has to go), I pull them out and make this syrup. It's tart and earthy from the ginger, and a tablespoon fancies up a glass of sparkling water beautifully.

MAKES 2 (HALF-PINT/250 ML) JARS

1 (12-ounce/340 g) bag cranberries
1 (3-inch/4.5 cm) piece fresh ginger, peeled and sliced
1 cup/200 g granulated sugar
Juice of 1 lemon

Prepare a boiling water bath and 2 half-pint/250 ml jars according to the process on page 11. Place 2 lids in a small saucepan of water and bring to a gentle simmer.

Place the cranberries, ginger slices, and 4 cups/1 liter of water in a saucepan. Place over high heat and bring to a boil. Lower the heat and simmer until the cranberries pop and release their flavor and color into the water.

Position a fine-mesh sieve over a bowl and pour the cranberries and their juice through it. Let the cranberries sit for at least an hour so that all the juice drips from the berries and into the bowl. Pressing the berries will make the syrup cloudy, but if that doesn't concern you, press away.

Rinse out the saucepan and pour the strained cranberry juice into it. Add the sugar and lemon juice. Bring to a boil and cook, stirring regularly, until a candy thermometer reads 218°F/204°C.

Funnel the syrup into the prepared jars, leaving 1/2 inch/12 mm of headspace. Wipe the rims, apply the lids and rings, and process in a boiling water bath for 10 minutes (see pages 11–12).

Spicy Apple Cider and Mustard Glaze

My kitchen is all of 80 square feet and my refrigerator is equally petite. Although I like to buy half-gallon of apple cider at the farmers' market, there's rarely enough real estate in my fridge to keep it for long. My solution is to cook the cider down so that I can enjoy the apple flavor without devoting too much of my precious fridge space to its storage. This particular glaze was inspired by a similar treatment in *The Mile End Cookbook*. Mine is tangier and spicier and holds up really well when paired with chicken or pork.

MAKES 3 (HALF-PINT/250 ML) JARS

8 cups/2 liters fresh unfiltered apple cider

1 cup/340 g honey

$^1/_2$ cup/90 g mustard seeds (a mix of yellow and brown is fun)

$^3/_4$ cup/180 ml cider vinegar

$^1/_2$ teaspoon Aleppo pepper

$^1/_8$ teaspoon cayenne pepper

Combine the apple cider, honey, mustard seeds, vinegar, Aleppo pepper, and cayenne in a large, wide pot. Bring to a boil and cook at a low bubble, stirring only occasionally, for 21/2 to 3 hours, until you've reduced the starting volume of more than 10 cups/about 3 liters to just 11/2 cups/360 ml.

When the glaze is nearing completion, prepare a boiling water bath and 3 half-pint/250 ml jars according to the process on page 11. Place 3 lids in a small saucepan of water and bring to a gentle simmer.

When the glaze has finished reducing, remove it from the heat and funnel it into the prepared jars, leaving $^1/_2$ inch/12 mm headspace. Wipe the rims, apply the lids and rings, and process in a boiling water bath for 10 minutes (see pages 11–12).

Note: For the best flavor, use fresh pressed, unfiltered cider.

Winter Fruit Mostarda

Traditionally, mostarda is whole or sliced fruit that's been preserved in a mustard oil–infused syrup. The end result looks like innocent preserved fruit, but has the sharpness and sinus-clearing power of horseradish. Because mustard oil is hard to find in the United States, I've combined mustard seeds and a few pinches of hot pepper to replicate that arresting flavor. Try it with cold roast beef or aged Gouda.

MAKES 3 (HALF-PINT/250 ML) JARS

1 pound/460 pears, like Bartlett, Bosc, or Anjou
1 pound/460 firm, tart apples
1 cup/340 g honey
2 tablespoons yellow mustard seeds
2 tablespoons cider vinegar
$\frac{1}{2}$ teaspoon Aleppo pepper
$\frac{1}{8}$ teaspoon cayenne pepper

Prepare a boiling water bath and 3 half-pint/250 ml jars according to the process on page 11. Place 3 lids in a small saucepan of water and bring to a gentle simmer.

Combine the honey with 1 cup/240 ml of water and the mustard seeds, vinegar, Aleppo pepper, and cayenne. Bring to a boil over high heat.

While the syrup heats, peel, core, and slice the fruit into 10 to 12 segments per piece. As you cut each piece, slip it into the cooking syrup, so that the fruit never gets a chance to oxidize.

Once all the fruit segments are in the syrup, let it cook for an additional 2 to 3 minutes, until the apples and pears are starting to go translucent, but before they fall apart.

When the time is up, use a slotted spoon to transfer the fruit into the prepared jars. Return the syrup to the stove, bring it back up to a boil and cook for 15 to 20 minutes, until it has reduced by at least half and looks quite thick. Ladle the thickened syrup over the fruit, leaving $\frac{1}{2}$ inch/12 mm of headspace. Tap the jars gently to remove any air bubbles. Add more liquid to return the headspace to $\frac{1}{2}$ inch/12 mm, if necessary. Wipe the rims, apply the lids and rings, and process in a boiling water bath for 10 minutes (see pages 11–12).

Dilled Carrot Spears

These pickled carrots are my midwinter riff on the classic dilly bean. I make them in January, when the pickings are slim at the farmers' market and I need to bring some color into my kitchen. I like to chop them and toss them into a batch of tuna salad for brightness and pucker. They're also good to make in early summer, when the true baby carrots are just becoming available.

MAKES 2 (12-OUNCE/360 ML) JARS

1 pound/460 g carrots
1 cup/240 ml cider vinegar
1 tablespoon pickling salt, divided
1 teaspoon dill seeds, divided
$\frac{1}{2}$ teaspoon black peppercorns, divided
2 garlic cloves, divided

Prepare a boiling water bath and 2 (12-ounce/360 ml) jelly jars according to the process on page 11. Place 2 lids in a small saucepan of water and bring to a gentle simmer.

Bring to a boil a separate small saucepan of water in which to blanch the carrots. Peel the carrots and trim to fit the jars. Cut into thin sticks.

When the water comes to a boil, drop in the carrots and cook for 90 seconds. Remove the carrots from the water and run under cold water to stop the cooking. Divide the spices and garlic cloves between the jars and pack in the carrot sticks on top of the spices.

Combine the vinegar, 1 cup of water, and the salt in a small saucepan and bring to a boil.

Pour the boiling brine over the carrots, leaving $\frac{1}{2}$ inch/12 mm of headspace. Tap the jars gently to remove any air bubbles. Add more liquid to return the headspace to $\frac{1}{2}$ inch/12 mm, if necessary. Wipe the rims, apply the lids and rings, and process for 10 minutes in a boiling water bath (see pages 11–12).

Note: To make these without the canning step, increase the blanching time to 3 minutes. That's just enough cooking to ensure that they're tender enough to absorb the brine but still snappy. Store in the refrigerator for at least 24 hours before using.

Carrot Relish

Because carrots are available year-round, they're not always the first on a preserver's list of things to put up. However, having a couple of jars of this relish on the pantry shelf is a huge boon to a hurried dinner hour. That's because it works as either a condiment or a dead-simple side dish. Spread on sandwiches or served alongside chicken breasts, it brings color and flavor to the plate. Even my husband, who claims not to enjoy things with a decided pucker, can down half a pint.

MAKES 3 (HALF-PINT/250 ML) JARS

1 pound/460 g carrots, grated
$^1/_2$ cup/75 g seeded and shredded red bell pepper
$^1/_2$ cup/80 g minced yellow onion
1 jalapeño pepper, seeds and ribs removed, minced
1 tablespoon finely milled sea salt
1 cup/240 ml cider vinegar
$^1/_4$ cup/50 g granulated sugar
2 teaspoons yellow mustard seeds
$^1/_4$ teaspoon freshly ground black pepper

Prepare a boiling water bath and 3 half-pint/250 ml jars according to the process on page 11. Place 3 lids in a small saucepan of water and bring to a gentle simmer.

In a large bowl, combine the carrots, red bell pepper, onion, jalapeño, and salt. Toss together and let the vegetables sit for 1 hour, until you notice that the salt has drawn out a significant puddle of water.

Pour the vegetables into a colander and rinse briefly with cold water. Drain.

Combine the vinegar, sugar, mustard seeds, and black pepper in a medium saucepan and bring to a boil. Once it begins to bubble, add the vegetables. Stir the vegetables into the vinegar mixture and bring back to a boil. Lower the heat to medium and cook for 3 minutes, until the vegetables are beginning to soften and have lent a little color to the vinegar.

When the time is up, remove the relish from the heat and funnel into the prepared jars. Wipe the rims, apply the lids and rings, and process in a boiling water bath for 15 minutes (see pages 11–12).

Spicy Pickled Cauliflower

T hese are the pickles I turn to when my taste buds need to be reset. Sharply acidic and spicy, they clear out the gustatory remnants of rich meals and overly sweet desserts. I happily eat them straight out of the jar with my fingers, but if you're serving more civilized eaters, here's what you should do: Heap the florets in a small bowl and drizzle a tablespoon or two of good olive oil over the top. A bit of oil turns them from a basic pickle into an instant marinated salad to be served with some sliced rounds of baguette and creamy goat cheese. They're perfect with drinks or as a quick predinner snack.

MAKES 4 (HALF-PINT/250 ML) JARS

1 small head cauliflower (about 1$\frac{1}{2}$ pounds/680 g)

1 cup/20 ml cider vinegar

1 tablespoon finely milled sea salt

$\frac{1}{4}$ teaspoon cayenne pepper

1 small lemon, thinly sliced, divided

2 large garlic cloves, sliced, divided

1 teaspoon black peppercorns, divided

1 teaspoon red chile flakes, divided

Prepare a boiling water bath and 4 half-pint/250 ml jars according to the process on page 11. Place 4 lids in a small saucepan of water and bring to a gentle simmer.

Wash the cauliflower and break it into florets. In a large saucepan, combine the vinegar, 1 cup/240 ml of water, and the salt and cayenne. Bring to a boil.

Place a slice of lemon in the bottom of each jar and top with the garlic clove slices, peppercorns, and chile flakes.

When the pickling liquid reaches a boil, add the cauliflower to the pot. Stir until the brine returns to a boil and remove from the heat. Pack the cauliflower into the prepared jars and top with the brine, leaving $\frac{1}{2}$ inch/12 mm of headspace. Tap the jars gently to remove any air bubbles. Use a chopstick to dislodge any trapped air bubbles. Add more liquid to return the headspace to $\frac{1}{2}$ inch/12 mm, if necessary. Wipe the rims, apply the lids and rings, and process the jars in a boiling water bath for 10 minutes (see pages 11–12).

Pickled Oyster Mushrooms

My neighborhood farmers' market has a mushroom vendor. Each week, he brings everything from giant portobellos to the alien-looking enokis. On particularly lucky weeks, he has fresh, fragrant oyster mushrooms. This is my version of one that my Internet friend Charlotte McGuinn Freeman posted on her blog, *Living Small*, some years back. I always eat them just as she suggested, by removing the mushrooms from the brine a bit before serving and drizzling them with toasted sesame oil.

MAKES 4 (HALF-PINT/250 ML) JARS

1 pound/460 g oyster mushrooms
2$\frac{1}{2}$ cups/570 ml rice vinegar
1 small yellow onion, sliced
1 tablespoon pickling salt
1 tablespoon granulated sugar
$\frac{1}{4}$ teaspoon black peppercorns
2 bay leaves, divided
2 garlic cloves, peeled and sliced, divided

Wash the oyster mushrooms well and chop them into pieces.

Prepare a boiling water bath and 4 half-pint/250 ml jars according to the process on page 11. Place 4 lids in a small saucepan of water and bring to a gentle simmer.

Bring a large pot of salted water to a boil and simmer the oyster mushrooms for 8 to 10 minutes, until they're tender. Drain.

In a medium pot, combine the vinegar, onion, salt, sugar, and peppercorns. Bring to a boil. Add the mushrooms and cook at a low boil in the pickling liquid for 5 minutes.

Divide the bay leaves and garlic between the prepared jars. Pack the oyster mushrooms and onion into the prepared jars and top with the brine, leaving $\frac{1}{2}$ inch/12 mm of headspace. Tap the jars gently to remove any air bubbles. Use a chopstick to loosen any trapped air bubbles. Add more liquid to return the headspace to $\frac{1}{2}$ inch/12 mm, if necessary. Wipe the rims, apply the lids and rings, and process the jars in a boiling water bath for 15 minutes (see pages 11–12).

Note: Make sure your mushrooms are very fresh with a springy texture and a faint whiff of the sea.

Lemon, Parsley, and Garlic Salt

Some families believe that no dish is complete without Lawry's Seasoned Salt. Others subscribe to the power of Old Bay. My people worship at the altar of McCormick's California Style Garlic Salt (the one interspersed with flakes of dried parsley). Throughout my childhood it was our house seasoning and lived on the top of the stove next to the salt shaker and pepper grinder. It wasn't until I was well into my 30s that I learned five minutes of chopping and a couple of days of air-drying meant I could take fresh ingredients and transform them into a far more flavorful version of our beloved garlic salt.

MAKES 1 (QUARTER-PINT/125 ML) JAR

1 pound/460 g lemons (4 to 5 lemons)
1 bunch flat-leaf parsley
3 garlic cloves
2 tablespoons coarse sea salt

Using a rasp-style grater, remove the zest from the lemons. Wash the parsley well and strip the leaves from the stems (you don't have to meticulous, but you want more leaves than stems).

Place the parsley on a large cutting board and chop roughly. Add the lemon zest and chop the two together until well combined. Add the garlic cloves and salt and continue to chop until the lemon zest, parsley, garlic, and salt are well combined and chopped very finely.

Spread out this mixture on a plate and let it dry for 48 hours at room temperature. When it no longer feels moist, scrape it into a jar and use as you would any other flavored salt.

Note: This recipe is endlessly adaptable and can be made with just about any herb. Try it with cilantro leaves and lime zest, or add some fresh rosemary and thyme into the mix for a deeper herbaceous kick. For easy application, save an old spice jar with a shaker lid and fill it with your herb salt.

Butternut Squash Butter

I grew up eating mashed butternut squash as a regular dinner-time side dish. Seasoned with butter and garlic salt, it was one of my mom's favorite things and so we ate a lot of it in the winter months. My favorite thing to do with butternuts (or any firm winter squash) is to roast them until the flesh is tender, spike it with a little sugar and warming spices, and cook it into a thick, spreadable paste. Stirred into oatmeal or spread onto toast with almond butter, it goes fast.

MAKES 3 (HALF-PINT/250 ML) JARS

1 medium-size butternut squash (3 to $3\frac{1}{2}$ pounds/1.4 to 1.6 kg)
$\frac{3}{4}$ cup/150 g granulated sugar
3 tablespoons cider vinegar
1 teaspoon ground cinnamon
$\frac{1}{2}$ teaspoon freshly grated nutmeg
$\frac{1}{2}$ teaspoon ground ginger
$\frac{1}{4}$ teaspoon ground allspice
$\frac{1}{4}$ teaspoon ground cloves

Preheat the oven to 400°F/200°C. Line a rimmed baking sheet with foil or parchment paper. Cut the butternut squash in half lengthwise (a few minutes of microwaving can make this an easier task) and scrape out the strings and seeds. Place the squash cut-side down on the lined baking sheet and roast for 30 to 40 minutes, until fork-tender.

Remove the squash from the oven and let it cool. Once you're able to handle the squash, scrape the flesh away from the skin. Purée the flesh in a blender or food processor until it's smooth. You should have $3\frac{1}{2}$ to $4\frac{1}{2}$ cups/860 g to 1.1 kg of purée.

Scrape the purée into a large skillet and add the sugar, vinegar, cinnamon, nutmeg, ginger, allspice, and cloves. Stir to combine.

Place over medium-high heat and cook for 25 to 30 minutes, stirring regularly, until the purée has reduced by about one-quarter and no longer looks watery. You know that your butter is finished when a scoop sits high and tall in the bowl of a spoon. If it's not done, it will run to the edges of the spoon and will be no higher than the rim.

When the butter is done cooking, remove it from the heat and spoon it into 3 clean half-pint/250 ml jars. Store the butter in the refrigerator for 7 to 10 days or in the freezer for up to 6 months. Because of its low acidity, this is not a product that be processed in a water bath canner.

Note: You can use any yellow winter squash for this recipe, including pumpkin. Just know that yields will vary, depending on the water content of the starting squash.

Caramelized Onion Spread with Sage

T his onion spread is a magical thing to make with winter storage onions. It is intensely savory and just a bit sweet. I like to keep a jar in the refrigerator for sandwiches or omelets. Make it while you're cooking dinner, let it cool while you eat, and purée it during cleanup. Truly, it could not be easier or more delicious.

MAKES 2 (HALF-PINT/250 ML) JARS

1 dry quart small yellow onions (about $1\frac{1}{2}$ pounds/680 g)
2 tablespoons unsalted butter
2 tablespoons granulated sugar
20 sage leaves, finely chopped
1 teaspoon finely milled sea salt
$\frac{1}{2}$ teaspoon freshly ground black pepper
$\frac{1}{2}$ teaspoon freshly grated nutmeg

Slice the onions into thin half-moons. Place a large skillet over medium-high heat and add the butter. Once it foams, add the onions and stir to coat. Cook over medium-high heat for 5 to 7 minutes, until they've started to relax into the pan and are easier to stir. Add the sugar, sage, salt, pepper, and nutmeg and stir to combine. Lower the heat to medium-low and cook, stirring regularly, until the onions have reduced by more than half and look quite brown and jammy, 45 to 55 minutes. As the onions cook, if they appear to be sticking or drying out, add a splash of water.

When the onions appear done, taste them and adjust the seasoning, as necessary. Scrape them into a large measuring cup and use an immersion blender to purée them into a chunky spread. Scrape into 2 half-pint/250 ml jars. The onion spread with last for 7 to 10 days in the refrigerator or up 6 months in the freezer.

Single-Quart Sauerkraut

Historically, people made their sauerkraut in large batches after the first frost because a freeze makes cabbage sweeter and slightly more tender. It would be packed into large crocks and allowed to ferment in a cool place. Here is my favorite way to make it in small batches without any special equipment beyond a wide-mouth 1-quart/1-liter jar and a cool, dark corner.

MAKES 1 (1-QUART/1-LITER) JAR

1 small green cabbage (about 2 pounds/910 g)
1 tablespoon finely milled sea salt
1 teaspoon caraway seeds (optional)

Wash a wide-mouth 1-quart/1-liter jar and a quarter-pint/125 ml jar.

Halve, core, and finely shred the cabbage. Place it in a large bowl and sprinkle the salt on top. Using clean hands, knead in the salt, squeezing firmly to help release the liquid from the cabbage. This should take 3 to 4 minutes. When the volume of cabbage appears to have reduced by half, add the caraway seeds and work them in.

Pack the salted cabbage into the prepared 1-quart/1-liter jar in layers, firmly pressing it down each time before adding more (the entire 2 pounds/910 g of cabbage should fit into a 1-quart/1-liter jar).

Press the cabbage down firmly in the jar, so that liquid bubbles up to the surface of the jar. Fill the quarter-pint/125 ml jar with clean water, put a lid on it, and fit it into the mouth of the larger jar. It will serve as a weight to keep the cabbage below the liquid level. Place a clean cloth over the top of the jar and secure it with a rubber band. Set the jar on a small plate or saucer, to catch any runoff, and place it in a cool spot out of direct sunlight.

Check your sauerkraut every other day, removing any scummy bloom and pressing the small jar down if any cabbage has floated above the liquid. Be forewarned, it will be a bit stinky. That's normal.

After 2 weeks, taste the sauerkraut. If you like the flavor, place the jar in the refrigerator. If you want something a bit stronger, let it continue to ferment until it pleases you.
Note: Ideally, you want to ferment your sauerkraut someplace that's between 60° and 70°F/16° and 22°C. If you keep your home below 60°F/16°C during the winter months, it will still ferment, but it may take longer.

Cross-Country Holiday Food Exchange

I come from a far-flung family. We stretch from the Hawaiian Islands to the very edge of the New Jersey shore. Aunts, uncles, and cousins are scattered throughout California, Pennsylvania, and Illinois. My sister lives in Austin, Texas, and my parents remain in our hometown of Portland, Oregon. Although I occasionally long to be part of a clan whose members are all within driving distance, having a family so dispersed has a number of upsides.

There's nearly always someone to stay with when you're traveling. Gatherings require time, planning, and funds, so they happen by choice as opposed to by obligation. And around the holidays, you can expect to send and receive at least a dozen boxes filled with homemade treats and local delicacies.

My California-based Aunt Lolly and Uncle Rob send jars of lemon curd made with eggs from their chickens and fruit from the tree in their yard. My dad preps bags of his signature pancake mix and pairs them with jars of my mom's wild blackberry syrup (always made from berries they picked themselves).

My cousin Harlan and his wife, Julie, are based in Hawaii and so pack up macadamia nut brittle and artistic treasures made by their kids. My uncle Mike orders wedges of aged Cheddar from a cheese-making friend in Vermont, while his brother Bill makes small hand-planed cheese boards for serving. Cousins Amy and Jean pack tins full of the miniature pecan pies called tassies, and chocolate and caramel-encrusted matzo.

Participation in this yearly cross-country food exchange is entirely voluntary. I didn't opt in until I was well into adulthood, but it's become one of my favorite things about holiday season. Thanks to my canning habit, most of my gift making is taken care of during the summer months. However, I do like to tuck something else into the box to go along with the jar of jam or chutney that I'm shipping off. In the past, I've made batch after batch of homemade crackers and quick breads to include with my jars. Through much trial and error, I've found that the best partner for my preserves is a small bag of slightly sweet, whole wheat shortbread. It's a good-tasting cookie that can be made quickly in large batches, and is sturdy enough to withstand the rigors of the U.S. Postal Service during the Christmas rush.

Whole Wheat Shortbread Cookies

MAKES 24 COOKIES

8 ounces/230 g (2 sticks) salted butter, at room temperature
$^3/_4$ cup granulated sugar
1 vanilla bean, split and scraped
2 cups/260 g whole wheat pastry flour

Preheat the oven to 325°F/170°C.

In the bowl of an electric stand mixer, cream together the butter, sugar, and vanilla bean seeds until the mixture is pale yellow and fluffy, and the vanilla seeds are well distributed throughout.

Add the flour to the bowl and run the mixer on low speed until the flour is just incorporated.

Turn out the dough into a 13 x 9-inch/33 x 23 cm rimmed baking sheet. Press the dough evenly into the pan and score with the tines of a fork.

Place the shortbread into the preheated oven and bake for 25 to 30 minutes, until the top is a light, even brown.

Run a butter knife around the edges to loosen the cookie. Place a larger baking sheet or cutting board over the top and invert the baking sheet. Using a sharp knife or pizza cutter, cut the shortbread into 2-inch/5 cm squares while it is still warm.

Let the cookies cool completely before packing in plastic and shipping.

Lavender Lemon Marmalade

very summer, my mom fills an envelope with lavender flowers from her garden and sends it to me. I know it's arrived the moment I walk into the mailroom, because the entire space smells fresh and clean. Because of these happy associations, I try and tuck lavender in any preserve that will have it. This marmalade is a particularly successful match-up.

MAKES 3 (HALF-PINT/250 ML) JARS

1 pound/460 g thin-skinned lemons
2 cups/400 g granulated sugar
1 tablespoon food-grade lavender buds

Wash the lemons in warm, soapy water and dry thoroughly. Using a very sharp knife, cut both the flower and stem ends off the fruit. Sit each trimmed lemon on one of its newly flat ends and cut it into 6 wedges. Lay each wedge on its side and cut away the strip of inner membrane and the seeds. Reserve the trimmed pith and seeds (we'll be using them as a pectin source).

Thinly slice each trimmed wedge. You want bits of lemon no more than $1/4$ inch/6 mm thick ($1/8$ inch/3 mm thick is even better) and $1 1/2$ inches/4 cm in length. Place the lemon confetti in a bowl and cover with 2 cups/480 ml of water. Bundle up the reserved seeds, inner membranes, and lavender buds into a length of cheesecloth, tie the ends tightly, and pop that into the bowl. Cover and place it in the refrigerator overnight (it can be left this way for up to 48 hours).

Prepare a small boiling water bath and 3 half-pint/250 ml jars according to the process on page 11. Place 3 lids in a small saucepan of water and bring to a gentle simmer.

Pour the lemons, pectin bundle, and water in a large pot. Add the sugar and stir to dissolve. Place the pot over high heat, bring to a boil, and cook for 15 to 25 minutes, until it reaches 220°F/105°C. The wider your pot, the faster it will cook. Once it has reached temperature and seems quite thick, remove the marmalade from the heat and discard the pectin bundle. Funnel the marmalade into the prepared jars, leaving $1/2$ inch/12 mm of headspace. Wipe the rims, apply the lids and rings, and process in a boiling water bath for 10 minutes (see pages 11–12).

Salt-Preserved Meyer Lemons

Meyer lemons are a cross between a traditional lemon and a tangerine. They are fussy to grow and don't travel particularly well, which can make them a little bit expensive if you live outside their preferred climate. Even if you can only afford a few of them, a little goes a long way, particularly when they're preserved in salt. Preserved lemons are traditionally a staple in Moroccan cooking. I use them in salad dressings, braises, and grain salads. They do good work in any dish that needs a little acidic funkiness and they last forever.

MAKES 1 (24-OUNCE/710 ML) JAR

1 pound/460 g Meyer lemons
$\frac{1}{2}$ cup kosher salt
1 cinnamon stick
$\frac{1}{2}$ teaspoon black peppercorns
$\frac{1}{2}$ teaspoon whole cloves
$\frac{1}{2}$ teaspoon allspice berries

Wash the lemons well. Trim away the stem end and slice the lemons into 6 segments per piece of fruit.

Place the spices in a large, wide-mouth jar (choose one that can hold at least 24 ounces/710ml). Pour 1 tablespoon of kosher salt into the bottom of the jar and pack in the first 6 slices of lemon. Top with salt and then more lemon and continue to alternate until the jar is filled and you're out of lemons.

Place a tight-fitting lid on to the jar and shake.

Let the jar sit in a cool, dark place for 2 to 3 weeks. Shake the jar daily to help distribute the salt, spices, and liquid. The lemons will have started out quite dry, but as they age, they should release enough liquid that the lemons are mostly submerged. Open the lid every few days, to allow the lemons to breathe and to release any fermentation pressure.

Once the lemon skins look soft and the liquid has taken on a pleasantly funky, tangy taste, put the jar in the fridge. They will keep up to a year.

Strawberry Meyer Lemon Marmalade

t happens every February. Standing in line my at local produce market with a basket of roots and greens, I smell strawberries. I buy a pound but, sadly, they're never as good as summer berries and so into the jam pan they go. Paired with a few Meyer lemons, the end result is a loosely set spread that evokes strawberry lemonade.

MAKES 4 (HALF-PINT/250 ML) JARS

1 pound/460 g Meyer lemons
1 pound/460 g strawberries
2 cups/400 g granulated sugar

Wash and dry the lemons. Trim off the ends and slice the fruit in half from to top to bottom. Using a sharp paring knife, cut out the pithy center core of each lemon half and remove the seeds. Reserve both the pithy cores and seeds (we'll be using them as a pectin source).

When all lemons have been trimmed, slice the halves into thin half-moons, place in a glass or plastic bowl, and cover with 2 cups/480 ml of water.

Gather up the reserved seeds and pith and tie them up tightly in the center of a cheesecloth square. Add this bundle to the lemon slices. Cover and set aside.

While the lemon slices soak, wash the strawberries and chop them well. Place them in a separate glass or plastic bowl and add the sugar. Stir to combine and cover.

Let both bowls sit for at least an hour and up to 3 hours. Stir the strawberries once or twice, if possible, to help the sugar draw out their liquid.

When you're ready to cook the marmalade, prepare a boiling water bath and 4 half-pint/250 ml jars according to the process on page 11. Place 4 lids in a small saucepan of water and bring to a gentle simmer.

Pour the lemon mixture and the strawberries mixture into a wide, nonreactive pan. Bring to a boil and cook over medium-high heat for 30 to 40 minutes, stirring regularly.

The marmalade is done when it reaches and holds 220°F/105°C, looks shiny, and is able to pass the plate test (page 000).

Funnel the finished marmalade into the prepared jars, leaving $1/2$ inch/12 mm of headspace. Wipe the rims, apply the lids and rings, and process in boiling water for 10 minutes (see pages 11–12).

Caramelized Meyer Lemon Syrup

Much like the pear caramel sauce on page 118, this recipe was born during a time when I was discovering that you could mimic a dairy-based caramel sauce with fruit. Because lemon juice doesn't have the substance of a purée, this recipe produces a syrup the consistency of honey. I love it drizzled over Greek yogurt or served with crisp waffles.

MAKES 2 (HALF-PINT/250 ML) JARS

Zest and juice from 1 pound/460 g Meyer lemons
$\frac{1}{2}$ teaspoon finely milled sea salt
$1\frac{1}{2}$ cup/300 g granulated sugar

Prepare a boiling water bath and 2 half-pint/250 ml jars according to the process on page 11. Place 2 lids in a small saucepan of water and bring to a gentle simmer.

Combine the sugar and salt with $\frac{3}{4}$ cup/180 ml of water in a separate small saucepan. Place over medium-high heat and simmer for 15 to 20 minutes, until the sugar reaches 350°F/180°C and darkens to the color of a tarnished copper penny. Do not stir the cooking syrup; instead, holding the handle of the pot, gently swirl it to move things around.

Once the syrup has reached 350°F/180°C, remove the pot from the heat and stir in the lemon juice. It will bubble, spatter, and appear to seize up, so take care. Stir until it is a smooth sauce and return the pot to the heat. Continue stirring and cooking until the lemon syrup reaches 218°F/104°C.

Remove the caramel from the heat and stir in the lemon zest. Funnel the caramel into the prepared jars, leaving $\frac{1}{2}$ inch/12 mm of headspace. Wipe the rims, apply the lids and rings, and process in a boiling water bath for 10 minutes (see pages 11–12).

Candied Meyer Lemon Slices in Syrup

his preserve is one of the most beautiful things I make each year. The thin slices of Meyer lemon are boiled until they are tender and have lost any sense of bitterness. Then they're bathed in sugar and cooked until translucent. You wind up with two jars of tangled, glowing lemon rind suspended in syrup. They are good in vinaigrettes, or arranged over the top of a simple cake. They make the perfect gift for cocktail lovers and home bakers.

MAKES 2 (HALF-PINT/250 ML) JARS

1 pound/460 g Meyer lemons
2 cups/400 g granulated sugar

Wash the lemons. Slice into rounds about 1/4 inch/6 mm thick. As you cut, poke out any seeds.

Prepare a boiling water bath and 2 half-pint/250 ml jars according to the process on page 11. Place 2 lids in a small saucepan of water and bring to a gentle simmer.

Place the lemon slices in a medium saucepan and cover with water. Bring to a boil and cook for 20 to 25 minutes, until the zest appears tender. Drain.

In a large saucepan, combine the sugar with 1 cup/240 ml of water and bring to a boil. Once the syrup is bubbling, add the lemon pieces and simmer until the rinds begin to look translucent, 10 to 15 minutes.

When they are sufficiently tender, use a slotted spoon to transfer the lemon slices to the prepared jars, then funnel in the syrup, leaving $\frac{1}{2}$ inch/12 mm headspace. Wipe the rims, apply the lids and rings, and process in a boiling water bath for 10 minutes (see pages 11–12).

Kumquat Marmalade

I f you live outside California, Texas, or Florida, kumquats
might not come your way often. And that's a shame, because they are
truly one of the most delightful members of the citrus family. They
reverse normal citrus behavior by being sweet on the outside and unre-
lentingly puckery on the inside. People in the know eat them whole,
candy them, pickle them (see page 174), and sliver them into batches of
marmalade like this one.

MAKES 2 (HALF-PINT/250 ML) JARS

1 pound/460 g kumquats
1$\frac{1}{2}$ cups/300 g granulated sugar

Prepare a small boiling water bath and 2 half-pint/250 ml jars according to the
process on page 11. Place 2 lids in a small saucepan of water and bring to a gentle
simmer.

Wash the kumquats well. Cut off the stem end and slice the kumquats into quarters.

When all the kumquats are quartered, use a sharp paring knife to cut away the
inner membrane and any seeds. Reserve the membrane and seeds, as they will pro-
vide the pectin. What remains will be a small piece of rind with some pulp still
attached. Lay these stripped quarters rind-side up and chop them into ribbons.

When all the chopping is done, you should have about 2 cups/300 g of chopped
kumquat bits, and a scant cup/130 g of reserved seeds and membrane. Place the
seeds and membrane in the center of a square of cheesecloth and tie it well.

Place the chopped kumquats, 2 cups/480 ml of water, and the sugar in a large pot.
Pop the bundle of seeds and membranes in, too.

Bring to a boil and cook for 15 to 25 minutes, until the mixture reaches 220°F/
105°C. The wider your pot, the faster it will cook. Once it has reached temperature
and seems quite thick, remove the marmalade from the heat (see note about check-
ing for set on page 14). Funnel the marmalade into the prepared jars, leaving $\frac{1}{2}$
inch/12 mm of headspace. Wipe the rims, apply the lids and rings, and process in a
small boiling water bath for 10 minutes (see pages 11–12).

Note: If your regular grocery store doesn't carry kumquats, pay a visit to your local
Asian market. They nearly always have a more diverse array of citrus than the main-
stream supermarkets.

Pickled Kumquats

Pickled kumquats are sweet, piquant, and surprisingly versatile. They are perfect with a triple crème cheese, cured or roasted meat, or with hearty green salads. Once the fruit is gone, stir the syrup into sparkling water, a cocktail, or vinaigrettes.

MAKES 2 (HALF-PINT/250 ML) JARS

1 pound/460 g kumquats
$1\frac{1}{2}$ cups/360 ml distilled white vinegar
$\frac{1}{2}$ cup/100 g granulated sugar
1 teaspoon pickling salt
6 peppercorns
6 whole cloves
2 cardamom pods
1 star anise
1 thin slice fresh ginger

Prepare a boiling water bath and 2 half-pint/250 ml jars according to the process on page 11. Place the lids in a small saucepan of water and bring to a gentle simmer.

Wash the kumquats and pick over for any that have soft spots. Using a sharp paring knife, trim off the stem end and cut the kumquats in half. Pop out any visible seeds with the tip of your paring knife.

Place the halved kumquats in a separate small saucepan and cover with cold water. Bring to a boil and then turn off the heat. Let the kumquats sit for 5 minutes. When the time is up, pour the kumquats into a colander. Wipe out the saucepan and add the vinegar, sugar, and salt.

Place the spices in the center of a length of cheesecloth or in a tea infuser and add to the liquid. Bring to a boil.

Once the pickling liquid has come to a boil, add the softened kumquats. Simmer for 1 to 2 minutes.

Remove the pot from the heat and funnel the kumquats into the prepared jars, leaving $\frac{1}{2}$ inch/12 mm of headspace. Tap the jars gently to remove any air bubbles. Add more liquid to return the headspace to $\frac{1}{2}$ inch/12 mm, if necessary. Wipe the rims, apply the lids and rings, and process in a boiling water bath for 10 minutes (see pages 11–12).

Orange Cardamom Curd

uring the late winter months, I go a little crazy for citrus. I order lemons from California, snap up boxes of clementines, and fill bowls with sweet navel oranges. Of course, I always overbuy. Last winter, I needed to use up extra few oranges, so I determined to make curd for an upcoming brunch. This recipe was the result and it is particularly good spread on buttered whole wheat biscuits.

MAKES 2 (HALF-PINT/250 ML) JARS

3 medium-size navel oranges (about 1 pound/460 g)
1 cup/200 g granulated sugar
1 teaspoon ground cardamom
6 large egg yolks
6 tablespoons cold unsalted butter, cut into cubes

Fill a medium saucepan with 2 inches/5 cm of water and bring to a low boil.

Remove the zest from the oranges with a rasp-style grater and place in a stainless-steel or tempered glass bowl that fits snugly into the heating saucepan. Cut the oranges in half and juice them until you have 1¼ cups/300 ml of orange juice. Add the orange juice, sugar, cardamom, and egg yolks to the zest and whisk. Once the mixture is mixed well, set the bowl on top of the saucepan. Switch to a silicone spatula and stir continually as the orange curd begins to cook.

As you stir, monitor the temperature of the curd with a candy or instant-read thermometer. The curd will begin to thicken between 190° and 195°F/about 90°C. Once it looks thick in the bowl and coats the back of a teaspoon, it is done. You don't want to let it cook beyond 205°F/95°C, as higher temperatures can cause it to curdle. Over medium-high heat, this curd typically takes 14 to 18 minutes to thicken.

When the curd has thickened, drop in the butter and stir until melted. Once the butter is fully incorporated, remove the curd from the heat.

Strain the curd through a fine-mesh sieve into a bowl. The straining removes both the zest (which will have imparted a great deal of flavor to the curd during the cooking time) and any bits of scrambled egg.

Pour the strained curd into 2 half-pint/250 ml jars for storage. When it has cooled to room temperature, store in the refrigerator or freezer. It will keep for 10 days in the fridge and up to 6 months if frozen.

Variation: Ruby Red Grapefruit Curd

During January and February, when the hefty Ruby Red grapefruit can be had for 50 cents apiece, I stock up. I eat them like oranges, juice them for cocktails, and make marmalades and jams. And plus, one curd is never enough for me. Omit the cardamom and replace the oranges with 2 medium-size Ruby Red grapefruit. Proceed with the directions for the orange curd.

Note: If you plan to freeze your curd, make sure to leave plenty of headspace, so that when it expands, it doesn't cause breakage.

ACKNOWLEDGMENTS

Like all those that have come before, this book was not a solitary effort. It was shaped, edited, named, and made beautiful through the efforts of many. My gratitude to this vast collection of people knows no bounds.

Thank you to my agent, Clare Pelino. She is just the right combination of tough and kind and has an uncanny ability to know whether I need encouraging words or a kick in the butt.

A mountain of gratitude goes to my editor, Kristen Green Wiewora. She has shown me that one can be both a valued colleague and a dear friend. I am so lucky to get to make books with her.

Thanks to Amanda Richmond, for once again styling and designing a book that I am delighted to call mine (and for working in a goodly amount of turquoise this time around). Steve Legato, thank you for taking my motley assortment of jars and preserves and transforming them into art. Mariellen Melker, thank you for gathering so many pretty things with which to enhance those images.

My parents, Leana and Morris McClellan, deserve a mountain of thanks. They helped me brainstorm flavor combinations, answered many a freaked freaked-out phone call, and read every word of this book when it was still rough and unformed. Truly, I think I won the parent lottery.

My sister Raina Rose and brother-in-law Andrew Pressman; I am so grateful to have you both as family and fellow travelers on this creative path. Also, thanks for bringing Emmett into the world. He is a spectacular kid.

So many thanks go to my husband and fellow writer, Scott McNulty. His unwavering love and steadfast belief in my abilities keep me moving forward, even when my own foundation gets a little shaky.

Many thanks go to my team of volunteer recipe testers: Christina Burris, Jennifer Downing, Jessica Diettrich, Rebecca Gagnon, and Christine Burns Rudalevige. These wonderful women jumped in and gave a number of my recipes a thorough going-over. This book is better for their efforts.

Finally, my unending thanks go out to the community of canners who read the blog, use my recipes, and share their many preserving successes. You all are the reason I do what I do.

INDEX

Note: Page references in *italics* indicate photographs.

Preserving Notes

Preserving Notes